TUITION REBATE

When Children Do Something Wonderful, It's a Return on Investment

Patrick McCaskey

A Sports and Faith Series Book

Sporting Chance Press™, Inc.
1074 Butler Drive
Crystal Lake, IL 60014
sportingchancepress.com

The photographs and illustrations appearing in *Tuition Rebate* were sourced from the Library of Congress, University of Notre Dame Athletic Department, Catholic Radio WSFI, Notre Dame College Prep, William Potter, Nikki Biese, Chicago Bears Football Club, U. S. Army, U. S. Air Force, U. S. State Department, Sporting Chance Press, and Wikimedia Commons. Please see the Photographs and Illustrations Credit Table beginning on page 188 for more information.

The opinions and ideas expressed are those of the author who is entirely responsible for its content. The author has composed *Tuition Rebate* at his own expense, using his own resources and technology. This publication is not associated in any way with the Chicago Bears Football Club, Inc.

Tuition Rebate is Book 6 of the Sports and Faith Series.

TUITION REBATE

I went to school for a long time.
It cost my family a lot of money.

Patrick McCaskey

Sporting Chance Press Books
by Patrick McCaskey

Sports and Faith: Stories of the Devoted and the Devout

Sports and Faith: More Stories of the Devoted and the Devout

Pillars of the NFL: Coaches Who Have Won Three or More Championships

Pilgrimage

Worthwhile Struggle

Sportsmanship

Papa Bear and the Chicago Bears Winning Ways

Poems About the Gospel

Poems About the Gospel II

Tuition Rebate: When Children Do Something Wonderful, It's a Return on Investment

CONTENTS

Patrick McCaskey

COMMITMENT

If we take up the Cross, we will find life.
Let us forget ourselves, even in strife.

— PKPMc

From our earliest days as children, we learn about commitment from our parents, siblings, teachers, and coaches. I often refer to these wonderful people in my writing. They have blessed my life.

With good guides in our youth, we commit to a faithful life. We commit to a good marriage, a good family, a worthwhile career, and so much more. At many points in our lives, we are challenged to live out our faith. This can be difficult.

Examples from sports help clarify what's involved. We know that a competitive athlete commits to exercise, diet, and acquiring the knowledge and skills that will lead to success. Like the athlete commits to sport, we commit ourselves to our responsibilities and those around us with discipline.

Mike McCaskey

Mike McCaskey was the oldest grandson of George Halas and the firstborn son of Edward and Virginia McCaskey. He would serve the Bears for three decades, but that was not planned.

In 1960, Presidential Candidate John F. Kennedy stopped along the campaign trail at the University of Michigan. He challenged students by asking who of them would be willing to live in underdeveloped countries to help people better meet their needs. The future "ask not what your country can do for you—ask what you can do

1

for your country" President wanted to see young people commit to serve, not to be served. The following year, President Kennedy signed an executive order establishing the Peace Corps. Kennedy's words struck a chord all over the world with the young.

After Mike McCaskey had graduated from Notre Dame High School in Niles, he attended Yale University and earned degrees in philosophy and psychology. In the early years of the Peace Corps, McCaskey signed up for a two-year assignment, teaching science and English in the town of Fiche in central Ethiopia. Although his work there might only be found in a footnote in a story on McCaskey, his experience there and continuing commitment to the area would always be important to him. He was not a student in Ethiopia, but when he was there, it was a time of great learning and discovery.

Mike McCaskey with Children from Fiche

After his Peace Corps experience, McCaskey obtained a Ph.D. in business from Case Western Reserve University. Then he set off on a college teaching and research career that followed at UCLA and Harvard Business Schools for over a decade.

Meanwhile, George "Mugs" Halas Jr. had unexpectedly died in 1979 after serving as Bears Treasurer, President, and General Manager. Mugs might have taken the Bears into the 21st century. When George Halas, Sr. died in 1983, Virginia McCaskey became principle owner and her husband Ed McCaskey became Chairman of the Board. Family members urged Mike to return to Chicago. McCaskey complied and served the Bears, first as President and CEO, and then as Chairman. During that time, the Chicago Bears won the 1986 Super Bowl XX (1985 Season) and the team was ranked as one of the best in NFL history.

Mike McCaskey died June 15, 2021, after a long battle with cancer. Current Bears President and CEO Ted Phillips said: *"Michael always strived to do things the right way with high character and with the Bears best interests always paramount."*

Memories of Michael Benning Patrick McCaskey by the Author

More than ten months after my parents' wedding, my brother Mike was born in Pennsylvania. He was wrapped in an army blanket and laid in an open footlocker.

When I was in second grade at Saint Mary's School in Des Plaines, I was in Sister Amata's class. Mike was going from Saint Mary's to Quigley Preparatory Seminary. I said to Sister Amata, "There isn't enough paper to write all the good things about my brother

Mike." At the end of the school year, Sister Amata gave me a stack of paper about a foot high. On the top of the stack was a note from her. "Here is some paper to get you started on writing about your brother Mike."

There is nothing like a nun.

In the summer of 1964, I was going to be a sophomore at Notre Dame High School and Mike was going to be a senior at Yale. I wanted to be a quarterback, and Mike wanted to be a receiver. So, we worked out together.

At one point, I called for Mike to run a two-yard square out. After the play went for an incompletion, he said to me, "You're calling out the signals in a loud, clear voice, but no receiver in the world can catch a two-yard square out when you throw it that hard."

In the summer of 1967, I had to give up playing football because of severe eye problems. I quietly put my newspaper clippings and trophies in the garbage. Mike and my mother later retrieved them.

Many of the McCaskeys and the Quinns attended Catholic grade school together. Friendships developed between us that lasted beyond our school days. Mike and I would go over to the Quinns' home every Christmas. We were known as the ghosts of Christmas past. For Christmas of 1971, we stayed until dawn.

When I got married in 1984, Mike served as my best man. When my son Jim was baptized in 1991, Mike was the godfather.

Here is my last phone message to Mike.[1]

Hello Mike. This is Pat McCaskey. I'm very sorry about your condition. Thank you for being my brother and my best man. It was always great to be with you, especially when we went to the Quinns as the ghosts of

---

[1] Mike McCaskey died during the coronavirus epidemic.

TUITION REBATE

*Christmas past. I look forward to being with you
again, on the other side. Goodbye Mike.*

Remembering Mike McCaskey by His Friend, Tom Fahey

I have been a friend of Mike's for over 70 years.
Inasmuch as I was an only child, Mike became the
brother I never had.

Who was Mike?

Certainly, he was a son, a father, a brother, an uncle,
a friend: but he was much more. I am reminded of the
parable of the three blind men each touching a part of an
elephant and then describing what they envisioned the
elephant to be.

Mike was a Renaissance man—a man of many
talents. He was a student, a teacher, a businessman, a
philanthropist, a photographer. One of the highlights of
his life was having one of his photos published in "The
New York Times."

He was competitive—Lord did he hate to lose. He
was analytical in evaluating situations and was always
measured in his response. This applied to his golf game,
personal life, and business dealings.

When asked a question, he would often begin an
answer, but would then ask, "What do you think?"

He certainly could enjoy a humorous story or event
and would reward it with a hearty laugh. He enjoyed
music and would often spontaneously break out in song.

His last words to me were, "I love you, pal."

The feeling was mutual.

We miss you, Mike!

5

Meseret Defar

Mike McCaskey was a fan of Meseret Defar. Defar was born on November 19, 1983, near Addis Ababa, Ethiopia. Raised about eight miles outside the capital city, she is the fourth of six children. The children walked about a mile to a river to get water. They loaded buckets and then they returned home. They took multiple trips. They headed to nearby woods to stock a wood-burning stove.

Defar began her running career in primary school. Defar and her husband, Tewodrus Hailu, met at an athletic club. He was a soccer player. Then he became her coach. They got married shortly before the 2004 Olympic Games. They have two adopted daughters and one by birth.

Meseret Defar has won three medals in the Olympic 5,000-meter run: the gold medal in the 2004 Athens Olympics, the silver medal in the 2008 Beijing Olympics, and the gold medal in the 2012 London Olympics.

After she had won a gold medal in Athens, she was appointed as the United Nations Goodwill Population Fund Ambassador to Ethiopia. She has consistently used the celebrity she has earned winning gold medals and breaking world records to highlight the needs of malnourished and impoverished children in the developing world.

Defar has won 13 world championship indoor and outdoor medals. She has set world records at 3,000 meters, two miles, and the 5,000. She is 5 feet, 3 inches tall and she weighs 95 pounds.

Defar donated her 2004 Olympic 5,000-meter gold medal to a church museum in Addis Ababa. Her 2012 Olympic 5,000-meter gold medal is on display in the hallway of her Addis Ababa home.

In the London Olympic final, Defar was in last place for most of the race. With four laps to go, she moved into second place. With 100 meters to go, she sprinted to win the gold medal. She ran the last lap in 62 seconds.

After Defar had won the gold medal in London, she fell to her knees. Then she held aloft an image of the Madonna and Child that she had hidden in her tank top. Defar wept and she kept repeating the Amharic words, "Amlake hoy! Amlake hoy! ("My God! My God!")

Sports and Faith at the Vatican

The Vatican holds many conferences each year. One of particular interest to sports enthusiasts was held in 2016 with the blessing of Pope Francis: "Global Conference on Faith and Sport." It was assembled by the United Nations, the International Olympic Committee, and the Vatican. This particular conference was referred to as "Sport at the Service of Humanity." Gathered were people from different religious faiths, sports, and related backgrounds who discussed how faith and sport can work together to serve humanity. Follow-up conferences have taken place at prominent American Universities. These involve athletes, religious, and related people. Faith and sports can work together to promote good values and help humanity. Pope Francis is keen on this idea and wants to see it spread.

Athletica Vaticana

Pope Francis, known as a huge soccer fan, encouraged the development of the Vatican's own sports team Athletica Vaticana in 2019. Acknowledging the importance of sports in everyday lives, Pope Francis said that sports can become a "sacramental of beauty."

The creation of Athletica Vaticana is a joint effort with the Italian Olympic Committee that leads the way to international sports. Teams are made of mostly citizens and employees of the Vatican, the world's smallest nation state.[2]

In 2021, the team was taking shape and joining up with various sports organizations and members started competing. At the marathon in Messina just weeks after the Athletica Vaticana's establishment, Father Don Vincenzo Puccio, a Sicilian priest, won a silver medal for the team.

On Tuesday, November 23, 2021, World Taekwondo officially recognized Athletic Vatican as the 211th member of the International Federation. The Korean Taekwondo team previously performed in Saint Peter's Square, in front of Pope Francis to affirm a message of peace through sport.

Athletica Vaticana marathoners look to compete against small European or Mediterranean countries. Perhaps the team will be in the Olympics someday.

Cycling is another sport of the association. Pope Francis and other Vatican leaders are quick to point out the many ways sports can help with inclusion and other values that are at the heart of Christianity. Sports can eliminate differences and improve understanding among different faiths and cultures.

---

[2] Inés San Martín, "Vatican official: Sports can help restart society after pandemic," ANGELUS, November 16, 2021. Viewed at https://angelusnews.com/news/vatican/vatican-official-sports-can-help-restart-society-after-pandemic/ on November 29, 2021.

Dinner with Jakeem Grant and Robert Quinn

Jakeem Grant is a receiver and a
Punt returner for the Chicago Bears.
We traded for Jakeem; he made the team.

In one quarter, he caught a forty-six-
yard touchdown pass and he returned a punt
Ninety-seven yards for a great touchdown.
He earned Special Teams Player of the Week.

Robert Quinn is an outside linebacker
For the Chicago Bears. He helps us win.
He earned Defensive Player of the Month.

He has gone from free agency to Bears'
Legacy. He is the Bears' sack master.

It was an honor to have dinner with
Them, Jakeem's family, and his agent.

Molly Seidel

Notre Dame Alum and decorated distance runner Molly Seidel won the bronze medal in the women's marathon at the Tokyo Olympics on August 6, 2021. Seidel is the third American woman to win an Olympic medal in the marathon. While it was only her third time running a marathon, the 27-year old has been winning distance races for many years. She made Team USA in February 2019 by placing second in the Olympic Trials, her first marathon!

Molly Seidel

When Seidel was in fourth place in a group of runners in the Olympic Marathon, she started to pray to Saint Jude, something that her mother and grandmother had done whenever things got tough. She was able to move into third and hold on until the finish.

Like many great distance runners, Seidel moved to train in weather that would approximate Tokyo's hot summers. She trained in Flagstaff, Arizona, and now lives in Cambridge, Massachusetts, near her sponsor, Puma.

A graduate of the University of Notre Dame in 2016, Seidel won many titles over her high school and college cross country and track careers. The Irish are proud of Seidel, the most decorated runner in Notre Dame History. Few Irish athletes have accomplished what this 5-foot-4, 107 pounds distance runner has done.

Seidel grew up in Hartland, Wisconsin. She was in fifth grade when she dazzled her gym teacher with her time for the mile. Running at University Lake School in Hartland, she won 12 state titles in high school track and cross country. When she visited Notre Dame, she felt at home when students asked her to go to Mass. But Seidel's first 2 years at Notre Dame were filled with sickness, injuries, and anxiety. Coach Matt Sparks never lost confidence in her and in time she came to believe in herself and her abilities.

In 2015, Seidel won the 10,000 meters in the NCAA Championship outdoor meet and she won the NCAA Championship in the 6-kilometer cross country event. In 2016, she won the 3,000 and 5,000 meters at the NCAA Championship indoor meet.

Seidel is committed to running. She continues to compete. On November 7, 2021, Seidel finished fourth in the New York Marathon. She wants to race in Paris at the next Summer Olympics.

Chicago Bears' Fans of the 1980s saw a lot of Matt Suhey

For Bear Fans, Matt Suhey is an old friend from a cast of great characters that was led by Walter Payton in the 1980s. Suhey was number 26. In honor of Suhey, I put turkey hot dogs in the microwave for 26 seconds. When I have turkey hot dogs, I think of Suhey.

Matt Suhey was born in Bellefonte, Pennsylvania, and he attended State College Area High School. He went to Penn State University—a school that continues to produce many of the best, toughest football players in America. His grandfather, Bob Higgins, was a Penn State alum who played end with the Canton Bulldogs in the first two seasons (1920 and 1921) of the NFL. Matt Suhey's father, Steve Suhey, was a Penn State alum who played guard for the Pittsburgh Steelers for two seasons (1948 and 1949).

Matt Suhey was drafted in the 2nd round in 1980. He played fullback with the Bears for 10 seasons through 1989. Suhey is remembered as the fullback who played alongside Walter Payton during much of the 1980s, including the 1985 Championship season that culminated with Super Bowl XX. Suhey was a team player who was superb at blocking for Payton. He had the stamina to play alongside "Sweetness" for eight seasons. Suhey was also a good friend of Payton's.

When Suhey ran with the ball, he gave the offense a "changeup." He had a splendid career with 828 career rushes for 2,496 yards for 20 touchdowns. As a receiver, he tallied 260 receptions for 2,113 yards and 5 touchdowns.

Jim Covert

If the Apostles had played football, they would have been a great team. James the son of Zebedee and his brother, John, were known as the "sons of thunder." They would have been the running backs like Walter Payton and Matt Suhey. We don't know much about Philip. So, he would have been a lineman like Jim Covert.

On August 7, 2021, Suhey presented Covert for induction into the Pro Football Hall of Fame.

Covert was a first-round draft choice of the Bears in 1983. He played offensive left tackle for the Bears from 1983 through 1990. He made the All-Rookie team. Covert won the Brian Piccolo Award. He was very active in the community, especially for S.T.O.P. (Sports Teams Organized for the Prevention of Substance Abuse). He played on the Bears' 1985 Championship team. He was a Bears' captain. He played in two Pro Bowls. He was All Pro twice. He made the NFL 1980s All-Decade Team. Covert is a Pro Football Hall of Famer. Here is his Hall of Fame acceptance speech.

"Thank you! Check that hair out, right? (Covert is glancing at his Hall of Fame bust.) It was the 80s, what can I say, right? I think Marino's hair got caught up on that.

"Thank you. Matt, I'm proud to have you as my presenter, even though you went to Penn State.

"And we tease each other all the time about that. I always say my favorite weekend is when Penn State, Notre Dame, and Green Bay all lose in the same weekend.

"Just kidding, Franco. Okay. Thank you, Matt. I really appreciate you being here for me.

"I want to thank all the staff here at the Pro Football Hall of Fame. David Baker and his staff are amazing. You made this an incredible experience for me and my family.

"Thank you to the Centennial Committee, especially Dan Pompei, and congratulations to the entire Centennial Class of 2020. I am proud to be inducted alongside you.

"Congratulations to the Class of 2021, who will be on this stage tomorrow night, and to the guys sitting all around here, the members of the Pro Football Hall of Fame. You're all my heroes. Thank you very much.

"And I want to say thank you to the Chicago Bears organization. Ted Phillips and the McCaskey family, and one McCaskey in particular, Ed McCaskey. Ed was a remarkable person who made Penny and me feel so welcome when we first got to Chicago.

"When I got hurt in training camp in '88 and had to go for back surgery, Ed visited me every day in the hospital. He bought me lunch from Tufano's, and he'd sit there with the Sportsman's Park racing form chewing on that cigar and say, "Jimmy, what do you think of this horse?"

"So growing up, I never dreamed I'd be standing here in front of you at the Pro Football Hall of Fame. And there are so many people that helped make that happen, starting with my mom and dad.

"And I always said I never had far to look for role models because they were right down the hall. My dad, like my grandfather before him, worked at ARMCO Steel in Ambridge, Pennsylvania, for 34 years.

"And I remember once he took me to the hot mill in July when I was like 10 years old and said, 'Son, you never want to come in here.' And one week a month, when he worked night turn, he'd come home early in the morning, change, and then go back out in a Sears and Roebuck moving truck for another eight hours delivering appliances. And as a kid, that makes quite an impression on you.

"My mom is my biggest fan. Right there. There she is.

"No one can say anything about her kids. No one. She worked at JC Penney part time in Northern Lights Shopping Center in Baden.

"Anyone remembers that. We called it 'JC Pennay' to make it sound more exotic.

"We got that discount. The husky section, right, Mom? Every single time.

"Yeah, my mom is the rock of our family. Thank you, Mom. I love you. Thank you for everything.

"I'd like to thank my beautiful wife, Penny, sitting right down there in front.

"She's had to put up with so much, most of all being married to me. But all the injuries and surgeries, even helping me to the bathroom some Monday mornings, all the while raising our family. Honey, you're the glue that holds us together. Thank you. I love you so much. Thank you. Thank you.

"And I have three great kids: Casey, Jessica, and Scott. I'm proud of each of you. Each one of you. Thank you.

"I'd like to thank my sisters, Deb and Elaine, and my brother, John, for all their love and support over the years. And I promise this is the last thing you have to go to for me, okay? I really appreciate it.

"I grew up in a town in western Pennsylvania called Conway, PA. We have Conway people up there. I think.

"Yeah! It's still home. So right down the street, right down Route 65 is Freedom High School. I think the Bulldogs are up there I think on top. Go Bulldogs!

"I played for a guy named Chuck Lucidore. Chuck made you believe in yourself and your abilities and made football fun again. He's turned us into winners. He's no longer with us, but I owe him tremendous, a lot. I was very fortunate to play for the University of Pittsburgh. Hail to Pitt!

"Pitt is an incredible place, and I played with some of the greatest college football players of all time and with some of the greatest college football teams of all time. And many of my Pitt teammates are here tonight. Danny [Marino] is up here, Rick Trocano, Jim Morsillo, Emil [Boures], they can all attest to that.

"At Pitt I played for two great coaches in Jackie Sherrill and Joe Moore. And Jackie was a great player's coach who really cared about you as a person, not just a football player. When I moved to the offensive line in spring of '80, he took a personal interest in making sure it was the best move for me. Thank you, Coach Sherrill. I love you.

"And I owe so much of my success to Joe Moore who I consider to be one of the greatest offensive line coaches of all time. And after I switched to offensive line, the first practice, Joe said, 'You're going to be an All American someday.' Now, he could have said anything, but after he said that, I would have run through a brick wall for the guy.

"He was great to play for most of the time—and I got a lot of Joe Moore stories. I only got six—no, three minutes left so—but Joe just had a unique way of pushing you, even beyond your own expectations, and then he took great pride in seeing you succeed. So he's no longer with us, but thank you, Joe. I miss you. I owe you so much. So thank you.

"And finally, the Chicago Bears. When I first got to the Bears in 1983, we weren't a very good football team.

16

TUITION REBATE

One of my first meetings, Mike Ditka said, 'I got good news and bad news. Good news is we're going to the Super Bowl. Bad news is half you guys won't be there when we do.'

"But he pushed us hard, but I also believe he reestablished a pride back into the Bears organization; that playing in the NFL is a privilege and not a right, and that when you pull that Bears jersey over your pads and put on that helmet with that 'C' on the side, it means something special. So thank you, Mike. I appreciate it. Thank you.

"I had the opportunity to play with some incredible players. And when you talk about great Bear players, it all starts with Walter Payton. I can't tell you anything more about Walter, but I got—since I got a couple minutes, I'll tell one quick story about Walter.

"Back in the day, no one had single rooms. Everybody had to room together. But Walter had a single room, of course. He was the only one. Matt and I roomed together. His room was always next to ours.

"When it was a big game, every once in a while that door would fly open, and he would run in there and jump right on top of me. Right? And he'd lean down, you know he had that voice like Michael Jackson, you know, and he said, 'Good morning, sunshine...time to kick some ass!'

"He was the best. I wish he was here with us tonight.

"At practice I played against some of the best defensive players of all time. Richard Dent and I squared off against each other every day. Sometimes we didn't like each other very much, but we made each other better. Thank you, Rich, my brother. I appreciate it.

"And then when you look down the line, you had Dan Hampton, another Hall of Famer, and then Steve McMichael, who I believe should be in the Hall of Fame.

And we are all thinking about you tonight, Steve, and wish you were here.

"I just know I wasn't going to face anybody on Sunday better than I faced during the week, so thank you, fellas.

"And Dick Stanfel was my line coach, and I learned so much from Dick. Not only was he a great Hall of Fame football player and coach, but he was an even better person.

"And finally I want to thank all my Bears teammates. Many are here tonight. I saw them last night. And I thank you all for coming. It really means a lot to me.

"But in particular, my teammates on the offensive line. We were very fortunate that the same five of us played together for 7 years of my career. Mark Bortz, Jay Hilgenberg, Tom Thayer, and Keith Van Horne, I can't think of four better guys that I would rather line up next to on any Sunday. So thank you, guys. You're the best.

"And in closing, I'd like to thank all the Chicago Bears fans out there. Your support has really been appreciated. Thank you all. Thank you, God. God bless you all. Thank you."

Trace Armstrong

Trace Armstrong was born in Bethesda Maryland, but went to high school at John Carroll Catholic High School in Birmingham, Alabama. He played linebacker and defensive end. He attended Arizona State where he played on the defensive line and finished off his college career at the University of Florida. Drafted in the first round by the Chicago Bears, the 6-foot-4, 275 pound lineman played with the Bears from 1989-1994 as an every-down defensive end. While playing regularly in Chicago, he had 42 sacks and 392 tackles. He was traded to the Miami Dolphins in 1995 and played there for another six seasons. In Miami, they deployed him in more specialized situations as a pass rusher. He ended his career in Oakland. He had 106-career sacks and 622 tackles.

Armstrong was invited to the Pro Bowl in 2000. He was named one of the Top 100 Bears of All Time. Armstrong went on to get a law degree and he is today a popular sports agent especially at representing coaches. He was the President of the NFL Players Association from 1996-2004.

Henry Wadsworth Longfellow in Longfellow Square

Patrick McCaskey

BLESSINGS AND SORROW

Not enjoyment, and not sorrow,
Is our destined end or way;
But to march, that each tomorrow
Finds us farther than today.
                    —Henry Wadsworth Longfellow

There are blessings in life and there are great sorrows. One does not come without the other.

Charles Tillman

If Charles Tillman got any better at tearing balls out of the arms of the opposition, they would have had to outlaw such play in the National Football League.

You can say a lot about football players, their skills, their intelligence, and their courage, but perhaps the best way to describe Charles "Peanut" Tillman is "remarkable." Tillman spent much of his life moving around because his father, Donald, was a sergeant in the United States Army. People with that kind of experience often have a remarkable understanding of others.

Tillman and his wife had a very tough experience with a young daughter born with heart problems and requiring transplant surgery. That certainly must have helped mold his personal sense of mission and charity towards others. His training and work in playing in one of the most competitive environments on earth, have certainly defined his physical presence, discipline, and maturity. Today, this remarkable pro football player has become an FBI Agent!

Cornerback Charles Tillman played 12 years for the Chicago Bears (2003-2014) and he helped the team reach Super Bowl XLI. He was an All Pro in 2012. He was honored as the Walter Payton Man of the Year in 2013. For the Bears, Tillman intercepted 36 passes and ran them back 675 yards for 8 touchdowns. Tillman forced 42 fumbles. He had 875 tackles, 754 of those were solo tackles.

This Monster of the Midway is numbered among the Top 100 Bears of All Time.

Mike Brown

Mike Brown was born in Scottsdale, Arizona, and went to Saguaro High School. Brown was among the top defensive backs and running backs in the state. He attended the University of Nebraska where his play at strong safety was outstanding. In his senior year he was an Associated Press All American.

The Chicago Bears selected Brown in the second round of the 2000 draft. Brown played safety for the Bears from 2000-2008. His early career was outstanding, but then he experienced a variety of injuries that took their toll on him. Brown's teammates gave him high marks for his understanding of defensive play and positions. Certainly when he was not on the field, he was sorely missed. He was an All Pro in 2001 and invited to the Pro Bowl in 2005. For the Bears, he had 17 interceptions, 523 tackles, 8 forced fumbles, and 5 sacks. Brown was named one of the Top 100 Bears of All Time.

John D. "Bonesetter" Reese

John D. "Bonesetter" Reese was one of the most fascinating figures in sports, although he was really not a sportsman. He was one of the most fascinating figures in medicine, although he was not a physician. Reese fixed aches and injuries with his hands. Baseball history is loaded with references to Bonesetter Reese. Hundreds of football players used his services as well.

Bear fans will be interested in knowing that George "Papa Bear" Halas used the services of Bonesetter Reese on three different occasions. Twice while he was a student at the University of Illinois and again when Halas had injured his hip sliding into second base for the New York Yankees. These are mentioned in Halas's autobiography, *Halas by Halas.*

Bonesetter's practice was focused on treating those who labored in places like mills and factories quickly and cheaply. Before health insurance or any government benefit for those disabled, an injury could cause financial ruin to a family. Often, a visit to the bonesetter would allow a laborer to get back to the job immediately or within a short amount of time. The quick turn-around appealed to athletes as well, although Reese was often disappointed by athletes who didn't follow his instructions after treatment. Bonesetter would work with athletes if they showed up at his door, but he was always focused on getting laborers back on the job.

Reese's grandson, David Strickler, published a book on his grandfather called *Child of Moriah: A Biography of John D. Bonesetter Reese* in 1989.

Steve Kelley and Father Kapaun

In the fall of 1968, Steve Kelley and I were Indiana University Freshman Cross-Country teammates. He did a great impression of a praying mantis.

When we got tired of saying "Fire Up," we said, "Ignite Skyward" and "Kindle Aloft." In the spring of 1970, Steve was the Big Ten steeple chase champion.

After school he became the longtime cross-country and track coach at Fresno High School in California.

Steve sent me a book called *Korea P.O.W. a Thousand Days of Torment* by William Funchess of the 24th Infantry Division. Funchess was a member of Steve's brother Pat's Methodist Church in South Carolina. Funchess's story is one of heroism, courage, and fortitude. He and others, who had survived the war, worked towards sainthood for Father Emil Kapaun who did not.

On April 20, 1916, Emil Kapaun was born in Pilsen, Kansas. He graduated from Pilsen High School, Conception Abbey Seminary College, and Kenrick Theological Seminary. On June 9, 1940, he was ordained a Catholic priest of the Diocese of Wichita. Father Kapaun was an Army chaplain during World War II and the Korean War.

Here is Funchess's praise for his chaplain:

"Father Kapaun, a Catholic priest, was one of the greatest men I ever knew. Although I am Protestant, I loved him dearly. Father Kapaun offered comfort to the POWs all over Camp 5. A person's religious background made no difference to Father Kapaun as he administered to all. He offered last rites for anyone whenever he could. He participated in work details and was never too tired or busy to offer a prayer for a troubled POW."

Father Kapaun had a blood clot in one of his legs. He also had dysentery and pneumonia. In the last month of Kapaun's life, Funchess nursed the dying priest the best he could in their squalid circumstances. Kapaun led an Easter sunrise service on Sunday, March 25, 1951. He died on May 23, 1951, at the age of 35 in Pyoktong, North Korea.

Soldiers who were liberated from Korean prisoner-of-war camps in 1953 told of Father Kapaun's heroism and faith. On June 29, 2008, the opening ceremony for the cause for canonization was held at Saint John Nepomucene Catholic Church in Pilsen, Kansas.

In 2021, the Defense Department identified the remains of Chaplain Kapaun. They had been interred with other unidentified remains at the National Cemetery in Honolulu. His remains are now buried in the Cathedral of the Immaculate Conception in Wichita.

Awarded the Bronze Star for bravery in battle, Father Kapaun was awarded the Distinguished Service Cross for his actions during and after the Battle of Unsan. President Obama posthumously awarded Father Kapaun the Medal of Honor on April 11, 2013, the highest award given to a member of the military.

Ed McCaskey and Brian Piccolo

In the winter of 1966, my father met with Bears legendary linebacker Bill George who said that he was leaving the Bears. Bill asked my father to take care of this boy on the taxi squad, Brian Piccolo, because he's something special.

In 1966, during the off-season, my father was in New York for almost two weeks. During that time, Brian Piccolo was also in New York. Piccolo was working in a corporate training program. Nearly every night, my father and his friends Maxie Kendrick and Johnny Desmond, along with Brian Piccolo, would have dinner together. My father really got to know Brian.

In the summer of 1967, my father started working for the Bears as the liaison among the owners, coaches, and players. His first day on the job, Brian Piccolo came to him and said, "Don't worry, Big Ed. I'll square you away with the players." He did and my father had a special affection for him.

Tough Goodbyes

All those who work in team management will tell you that it is especially painful when they have to say goodbye to players. After all, there are no "expiration dates" that come with players when they sign on. Personnel decisions are made with the best interest of the team, but they often are based on negotiations and deciding factors judged by human beings. Teams are not run on algorithms. But for most of the players, life goes on after their stay on the Bears roster. But for any team, there can be some very tough and tragic goodbyes. Like many other teams, the Chicago Bears have seen their share of tragedy, but the one that comes to mind for many Bears football fans is the tragic illness and death of Brian Piccolo.

Brian Piccolo

Brian Piccolo led the nation in rushing as a senior at Wake Forest in 1964 beating out his future teammate Gale Sayers. But at 5 feet 11 and 190 pounds, he wasn't very big; scouts also considered him too slow to draft. Nevertheless, he tried out for the Bears as a free agent and he earned a position on the taxi squad. In 1967, he saw increased action as backup to Gale Sayers, and the two became close friends when they became the first integrated roommates in the NFL. Piccolo took over for Sayers the following year when Sayers went down with a knee injury. He unselfishly supported and helped Sayers in his recovery.

When Sayers returned to play in 1969, Piccolo was once again relegated to the bench until he started in the backfield with Sayers. Then Brian developed a cough that led to medical tests and a diagnosis of lung cancer.

As Piccolo was battling the disease, Sayers won the NFL rushing title and also received the George Halas Award as the league's most courageous player for the 1969 season. At the award ceremony, Sayers suggested that the most courageous player in the NFL was his roommate and friend Brian Piccolo who "has the mental attitude that makes me proud to have a friend who spells out the word courage 24 hours a day, every day of his life."

"Brian is the man of courage who should receive the George Halas Award. I accept it tonight and I'll present it to Brian tomorrow."

Brian succumbed to lung cancer on June 16, 1970, and his life story and the Sayers-Piccolo friendship has been immortalized in the film "Brian's Song." Brian's wife, Joy Piccolo O'Connell, is a crusader in the fight against cancer.

Piccolo Award

Both a Bears' rookie and a veteran are selected by teammates for the Brian Piccolo Award each year. The recipients display the courage, loyalty, teamwork, dedication, and sense of humor exemplified by Piccolo. Piccolo is a Sports Faith Hall of Famer.

Before Brian's daughter, Kristi, spoke at the Brian Piccolo Awards Ceremony that acknowledged the 2020 Award recipients, I was confident that she would be eloquent, and she was.

Head Coach Matt Nagy also spoke.

Perhaps you wondered about Nagy's best game. In 1998, at the University of Connecticut, he completed 23 of 28 passes for 556 yards, 3 touchdowns, and one 2-point conversion. Delaware won 59-17.

When Tommy Lasorda was the manager of the Los Angeles Dodgers, his priority was to be upbeat, regardless of what had happened in the previous game. Lasorda was a lot like Nagy.

Nagy introduced Bears' receivers coach Mike Furrey. Furrey introduced the rookie Piccolo award winner, Darnell Mooney. Nagy introduced Bears' offensive coordinator, Bill Lazor. Lazor introduced the veteran Piccolo award winner, Allen Robinson.

Piccolo died in 1970. In 1973, his widow, Joy, married Rich O'Connell. That was fine with my father because he felt that O'Connell was an Irish Piccolo. At the ceremony, Joy came forth to accept a check from the National Football League to the Brian Piccolo Cancer Research Foundation for $50,000.

Willie Galimore and Bo Farrington

Often described as one of the most elusive runners in NFL history, Willie Galimore played halfback for the Bears from 1957-1963. He was 6-foot-1 and slim. Galimore was known for making quick movements in any direction that prevented tacklers from grasping him. Once he had an opening, he would head towards the goal while accelerating at uncatchable speeds. Mike Ditka said "he could fly."[3] Galimore attended Florida Agricultural and Mechanical University (FAMU), a top public historically black university where he rushed for 3,592 yards and set numerous records. He played seven seasons for the Bears and gained 2,985 yards on the

---

[3] Mike Ditka with Rick Morrissey, *In Life, First You Kick Ass: Reflections on the 1985 Bears and Wisdom From Da Coach*, (Champaign, Sports Publishing LLC, 2005) 102

ground and 1,201 yards receiving for a total of 4,186. He was called Willie "the Whisp" Galimore.

John "Bo" Farrington was born in DeWalt Texas and went to Jack Yates High School. He attended Prairie View A & M, a traditional black school that is the second oldest public institution of higher education in Texas.[4] He played receiver in college and was drafted in the 16th round of the 1960 draft by the Chicago Bears. He was a promising 6-foot-3 receiver who had been on the Bears for four seasons from 1959-1963. He had a 98 yard touchdown reception in 1961 that was tops for the year. Farrington played with Johnny Morris and Mike Ditka, two of the best receivers in football.

The Bears had won the 1963 NFL Championship. The team was strong and stocked with great players on both defense and offense. Halas described the Bears 1963 Championship as his "biggest personal satisfaction."[5] Things looked great for the Bears heading into their 1964 season. But tragedy struck.

On July 26, 1964, while the Bears were preparing for the College All-Star Game, teammates Willie Galimore and John "Bo" Farrington were killed in an automobile accident returning to camp after a day at a country club. The deaths shocked and saddened the Bears. Galimore left a wife and three small children. Farrington left a wife after just a few months of marriage.

George Halas called it the saddest day in Bears' history. In less than a year the Bears had gone from being

---

[4] History of Prairie View A & M University viewed at https://www.pvamu.edu/about_pvamu/college-history/ on November 16, 2021.

[5] Joseph S. Page, *Pro Football Championships Before the Super Bowl, A Year-By-Year History, 1926-1965* (Jefferson, NC: McFarland & Company, 2011)192.

national champion to mourning the loss of two teammates.

"Rabbit" Recovers and Is Redeemed

When a sinner repents, there is much joy.
—PKPMc

Walter "Rabbit" Maranville was a 5-foot-5 shortstop with tremendous athletic skills who played for 23 years in baseball's National League from 1912-1935 (except in 1934 due to injury).[6] Maranville covered a lot of ground out on the infield. He moved quickly from side to side and he leaped like a rabbit to snag high line drives—earning him his nickname. Decades before Willie Mays made basket catches of fly balls fashionable, Maranville was a master at it. He played for the Boston Braves, the Pittsburgh Pirates, the Chicago Cubs, the Brooklyn Robins, and the St. Louis Cardinals. If television would have been around then, the entertaining Maranville likely would have been a frequent guest on talk shows.

In the early days of baseball, many players came from the mines, the mills, and struggling farms where making a living could be brutal and relentless. They sought a better life. Games were played during the day and players traveled by train from city to city. Self-control could be a problem for young men who were on their own for the first time in their lives. There was plenty of dead-time, especially at night.

Maranville was a notorious clown. First, he drank too much. And he was a practical joker, a goldfish

---

[6] Sporting Chance Press's *The 10 Commandments of Baseball: An Affectionate Look at Joe McCarthy's Principles for Success in Baseball (and Life)* uses Maranville's story and others from baseball history to illustrate McCarthy's life lessons.

swallower, and a hotel-ledge walker among other things. Still, with his first team, the Braves, in five of his early seasons in Boston, the young Maranville led the National League in putouts four times, assists twice, double plays twice, and fielding percentage once.

Maranville's comic exploits were a joy for the press and a pain for his baseball managers trying to keep order. His hijinks caught up with him. He eventually moved around from team to team as managers lost patience with him. He hit rock bottom in 1926 before the legendary Branch Rickey of the St. Louis Cardinals picked him up and sent him down to the Minor Leagues to straighten himself out.

Maranville mended his ways and quit drinking. A year later, he was once again on top of his game, reunited with Boston. His stellar career continued. Five years into his return to Boston, the 42 year-old broke his leg and sat out the season in 1934. He retired in 1935. Maranville had come so close to ruining his career, but he turned himself around. His fielding records and longevity earned him a spot in the National Baseball Hall of Fame. Later in his life, he worked with young players and urged them to take a higher road than he had taken in his youth.

Ecclesiastes, Job, and Song of Songs

From Peter Kreeft's book "Three Philosophies
Of Life," we know that Ecclesiastes,
Job, and Song of Songs are played out in "The
Divine Comedy," Dante's great epic.

Ecclesiastes: life is vanity
From the Book of Job: life is suffering
From the Song of Songs: life is love. Amen.
From Hell to Purgatory to Heaven

Kreeft, "Ecclesiastes is the question...
The rest of the Bible is the answer."
Ecclesiastes is full of despair
Because he is not a Chicago Bear.

The singers in the Song of Songs sing well.
They're like Steve Lawrence and Eydie Gorme.

Biese Family

BIRTH

Mary was chosen to give birth to Jesus Christ.
She was His mother and His disciple.
She fulfilled the Father's will perfectly.

—PKPMc

With each birth, there are risks involved for mother and baby. Every life starts with uncertainty. Many other beginnings in life are followed by victory and success, or loss and failure.

We learn from all our beginnings, whether starting school, beginning a new job, or getting married, just to name a few. And with each step there are always more risks, more to learn, and promises that we need to keep.

Biking for Babies

Protecting the unborn is a crusade for people of faith today. There are many initiatives underway for this purpose. The effort to turn our society into one that respects life is being taken up by the young. This is encouraging, but they need financial help.

In 2009, Jimmy Becker and Mike Schaefer took their bikes to Southern Illinois University Carbondale to ride 600 miles, to fundraise, and to provide publicity for pregnancy resource centers. "Biking for Babies" (bikingforbabies.com) started because these young men chose to use the experience as a representation of the endurance and commitment young women and families face in unexpected pregnancy. They also raised over

33

$14,000 for a local pregnancy resource center! Pregnancy resource centers are places that offer tangible support and help—such as free pregnancy tests, ultrasounds, certain other medical tests, parenting classes, counseling, baby supplies, and much more.

Biking for Babies grew out of this effort with its founders' roots in FOCUS (Fellowship of Catholic University Students). At the forefront of the movement today are people like Executive Director Nikki Biese who states that Biking for Babies "believes in a world that responds to crisis with faith, hope and love. And in that world, there is no need for abortion." Nikki says Biking for Babies exists to answer Saint John Paul II's exhortation, "Woe to you if you do not succeed in defending life." There is no "choice" but to defend life; it is the 21st century battle for all people of faith as well as others who seek a civil society.

Certainly, there is a need to raise awareness to protect the unborn and a need to financially support pregnancy resource centers that care for women and their families.

With Biking for Babies, "each of the college students and young adults that have participated since 2009 have built friendships with each other, despite hardship along the way, and with those we have been honored and blessed to meet during our travels."

Advocates for Life

Biking for Babies efforts culminate in an annual National Ride where "Missionaries" bike into St. Louis from various cities. But this initiative isn't just about people who like to take long bike rides. Riders and support crew members enthusiastically apply to become "Missionaries." These young volunteers undergo a spiritual and physical formation program that lasts several months to prepare for the National Ride. The program brings young people closer to Christ, introduces them to a pregnancy resource center, and encourages them to advocate for their center. All of this is in order to bring about a renewal of the culture into one that supports life.

These rider and support-crew missionaries move on from the National Ride inspired and ready to impact their local communities. They are encouraged by their pro-life formation to go and spread the good news of the Gospel of Life, that all may know Jesus and see each and every life as a gift; a gift of immeasurable worth.

Biking for Babies accepts contributions in two ways: one for the support of the organization and its leadership efforts and another that comes from the supporters of the Missionary riders that goes directly to the partnered centers as well as the formation of the missionaries. There is nothing quick and easy about the efforts of Biking for Babies. But it is forming life-long advocates of a pro-life culture. It is also supporting the people and efforts at the centers that make a difference on the ground.

Joe Scheidler

On September 7, 1927, Joe Scheidler was born in Hartford City, Indiana. After he had graduated from Hartford City High School, he joined the U.S. Navy.

After Scheidler had been discharged from the Navy, he enrolled at the University of Notre Dame. Upon graduation, he took a job at the *South Bend Tribune.*

Scheidler went from South Bend to Our Lady of Lake Seminary in Wauwausee, Indiana, to the Benedictine Monastery at Saint Meinard to the Saint Thomas

Aquinas Center at Purdue University. Then he took a teaching job at the University of Notre Dame in the Department of Communication Arts. After that, he earned a master's degree at Marquette University.

In September 1963, he began teaching journalism and theology at Mundelein College in Chicago. When he was teaching at Mundelein College, he had accepted another job. The woman who would become his wife, Ann Crowley, was a senior at Mundelein College. She wrote him a note, "Don't go."

Scheidler declined the other job. On September 4, 1965, Joe and Ann got married. In 1966, Scheidler took a job with the city of Chicago Department of Youth Welfare. In 1972, he took a public relations job with Selz, Seabolt and Company.

In 1973, the Scheidlers started their pro-life activism. In 1980, they started the Pro-Life Action League. They won two cases before the Supreme Court of the United States.

In November 2016, his memoir of more than 40 years as a pro-life activist, *Racketeer for Life*, was published. He signed a copy to me, "Pat, God bless you for your dedication and support in saving our future children—and Bears' fans."

Shortly before Scheidler died on January 18, 2021, he said that he had felt fine until he heard that he was dying. His wife, Ann, said to him, "Thank you for reading my note."

On Monday, January 25, 2021, the funeral for Scheidler was at Saint John Cantius Church in Chicago. The burial was at All Saints Cemetery in Des Plaines.

Sports Faith Courageous Catholics

On April 27, 1919, my father, Ed McCaskey was born at the Jewish hospital in Philadelphia. His mother was Irish. She later told him that it had rained buckets all day long. Just as he was delivered, the sun came out and he accepted that.

Every baby deserves such love.

I have been blessed to work with many people who serve the underserved. It might be through church groups, the Chicago Bears, Civic organizations, various schools, and Sports Faith International that is affiliated with Catholic Radio WSFI 88.5 FM. Here are some of the best of the best who work to serve our most vulnerable.

Bonnie Quirke is a Co-Founder and President of Lake County Right to Life. She has served as the Illinois Director to the National Right to Life Board. She attends March for Life in Washington and Chicago. She and her husband, Jim, have six children and twelve grandchildren. She is an invaluable friend, supporter, and guest talk show host on WSFI 88.5 FM Catholic Radio.

Vicki Thorn is the Executive Director of the National Office of Post-Abortion Reconciliation and Healing, and Foundress of Project Rachel, a post-abortion healing ministry of the Catholic Church. She and her husband, William, have six children and 17 grandchildren. She received the People of Life Award for pro-life service to the Church. She is a WSFI 88.5 FM Healing Conference presenter on the Biology of Soul Ties.

Father Godwin Asuquo is the Founder of ImaBridge Africa which provides his homeland of Nigeria with healthcare, drinking water provisions, and education.[7] Since his ordination, he has served at Holy Angels Church, the Northern Illinois University Newman Center, and Marian Central High School in Woodstock. Now he is the pastor of Saint Patrick Catholic Church in McHenry.

Steven Westley Mosher was born on May 9, 1948, in Scotia, California. He grew up in Fresno. He has undergraduate and graduate degrees in Biological Oceanography from the University of Washington. After he had served in the Navy, he studied the Chinese language at Chinese University of Hong Kong. Then he earned graduate degrees in East Asian Studies and Anthropology at Stanford University.

In his book, *Broken Earth*, Mosher wrote about forced abortions in China to accommodate the one child policy.[8] He is the author of nine books and he and his wife, Vera, have nine children. He is President of the Population Research Institute, an internationally recognized authority on China, and a regular contributor to WSFI 88.5 Catholic Radio.[9] He is a convert to Catholicism. He is a pro-life activist.

---

[7] See organization website for more information: https://imabridge.org/

[8] Amazon listing for book: https://www.amazon.com/Broken-Earth-Steven-W-Mosher/dp/0029217202/ref=sr_1_24?keywords=%22Broken+Earth%22&qid=1637089386&s=books&sr=1-24

[9] See website of Population Research Institute for more information: https://www.pop.org/

Begins in the Womb

Life begins at conception.
We know equality begins in the womb.
Unborn babies deserve life and not a tomb.
We are here to follow God's direction.

God is always with us here on earth.
We are gathered here at Federal Plaza.
And everyone here seems to be saying
Life begins at conception.

To march for life again is our endeavor
Without exception we march with heart
And here we are, willing to march forever
God has inspired us to be so smart

What marching divine, what speakers serene,
Until time comes along to disperse us to the banquet.
And then when we hear all of us pray for unborn babies
We know all quite well what we mean

So, let's all follow God's direction
Let the love that God has shown the earth in creation
Let it inspire march for life be a great sensation
Life begins at conception.

Oh, we know equality begins in the womb
Because unborn babies deserve life and not a tomb
We march for life once more "Dear God, we love you!"
And we always follow God's direction
Life begins at conception.

March for Life Chicago

On Sunday, January 17, 2021, due to the Coronavirus disease 2019 (COVID-19), March for Life Chicago took place as a drive-in at the parking lot of Carmel High School in Mundelein. Here is the lineup of speakers:

- Archbishop Paul Grassios ruling hierarch for the Diocese of Chicago and the Midwest for the Orthodox Church in America.
- Brad Bonham, Ph.D. President of Carmel High School in Mundelein.
- Cardinal Blasé Joseph Cupich Archbishop of Chicago.
- Doctor Linda Couri on the Faculty at Mundelein Seminary.
- Hannah Arends President of Carmel Catholic's Pro-life club.
- Kevin Grillot Executive Director of weDignify.
- Margaret Pluta member of weDignify's chapter at the University of Illinois in Champaign.
- Mark Curran former Lake County Sheriff.
- Melissa Villalobos who was miraculously healed by the intercession of Saint John Henry Newman.
- Steve Lentz Mayor of the Village of Mundelein

weDignify

The grass roots pro-life organization called weDignify (wedignify.org/education/) helps college students become skilled, virtuous, pro-life leaders, so they can build and nurture a culture of life on campus and in their future communities.

The organization has a chapter at the University of Illinois and affiliates at DePaul University and Loyola

University. Its staff mentors students who become student leaders who in turn guide other students.

The weDignify organization prepares students to teach, serve, and lead within the pro-life cause. They teach in small groups but also through dialogue on campus.

The service part of the program is expanding to support pregnant women on campus. Students lead on campus and then as part of the March for Life Chicago volunteers and speakers. The March for Life Chicago is a program of weDignify that gathers people from throughout the Midwest in downtown Chicago to stand up for life.

Alumni are part of the weDignify community in that they volunteer for the March for Life Chicago and share their prolife beliefs in their professions and communities.

Melissa Villalobos and Saint John Henry Newman

In 2000, while getting ready for work one day, Melissa Villalobos, a wife and mother, first heard about Cardinal John Henry Newman on an EWTN broadcast. Drawn to the Cardinal's story, she discovered that Newman was born in 1801, later he became an Anglican priest, and then he converted to Catholicism in middle age. A year after Villalobos's introduction to Newman on EWTN, her husband brought her two holy cards of Newman. Devotion got stronger. Placing the cards where they could be seen, she found herself looking at Newman's image frequently. He seemed to be sympathetic to her moods.

Villalobos further investigated his life and writings. What impressed her was the Cardinal's tremendous regard for everyday people. Although Newman was an accomplished poet, an educator, a celebrated homilist, and someone who penned important works on religion and history of the Church, he never considered himself to be a theologian.

In 2013, more than a decade after first hearing about Newman on EWTN, pregnant with her fifth child, Villalobos was in trouble—bleeding continuously. She was diagnosed with subchorionic hematoma, a blood clot between the placenta and the uterine wall that causes the placenta to be partially ripped and detached from the uterine wall.

No medication or surgery could help; the outlook was grim—certainly it was a pregnancy that was unlikely to last through the third semester. The doctors prescribed strict bed rest, but Villalobos had four young children. On May 15, 2013, with her husband out of town on business, Villalobos woke up in a pool of her own blood. She struggled to look after her children's breakfast while she considered her options. Nothing came to mind. A short time later she collapsed on the floor, weakened by blood loss. She franticly called out to someone who might help, Cardinal Newman. "Please Cardinal Newman, make the bleeding stop."

Immediately the bleeding ceased and she felt at peace. The traditional scent of holiness, roses, filled the air. Later that day, Villalobos had an ultrasound, the bleeding had stopped. Her baby looked perfect. All this according to Villalobos through Cardinal Newman's intercession.

According to Villalobos, "Thanks be to Cardinal Newman and to God that I was cured and Gemma was born completely healthy."

After baby Gemma was born healthy, Villalobos reported the miracle to Father Ignatius Harrison, the postulator for Newman's cause for canonization and the Provost of the Birmingham Oratory (which Newman established). Harrison came to Chicago to investigate. He told Villalobos to keep things quiet while the analysis was ongoing. In February 2019, Villalobos received the news that Pope Francis signed the decree recognizing the miracle. Villalobos and family traveled to Rome for Newman's canonization on October 13, 2019.

Father Javier del Castillo

"Every Christian can and should be a living expression of faith."

Saint Josemaria Escriva

Father Javier del Castillo is a priest of the Prelature of Opus Dei. He has an Electrical Engineering degree and a Doctorate in Philosophy. He carries out his pastoral ministry in Chicago and is Vice President of the Saint Josemaria Institute. On Thursday, January 28, 2021, Father Javier del Castillo spoke to the Chicago Legatus Chapter about his family's adventures and trials securing a future here in the United States.

Saint Josemaria Institute

Saint Josemaria Escriva (1902-1975) was a Spanish diocesan priest who founded Opus Dei. Opus Dei fosters among Christians the search for holiness in the world, especially in the ordinary circumstances of life and the sanctification of work. To that end, Saint Josemaria helped others discover a new awareness of the dignity of the Christian vocation and to live the spirit of the Gospel more fully.

The Saint Josemaria Institute (stjosemaria.org/) promotes Saint Josemaria Escriva's life and teachings to increase devotion to him. It produces digital and print media inspired by Saint Josemaria. Through programs and resources, the Institute aims to help others become living expressions of faith and enjoy life as Christians.

Thoughts on Nate and Angela

Angela is a cancer survivor and the daughter of Wayne and Anne Gordon of Lawndale Community Christian Church (LC3) in Chicago.

Nate & Angela Celebrate Life

A life without strife is no life at all.
The important thing is answer God's call.

Life celebration is why we are here.
Nate & Angela deserve a big cheer.

They live the Gospel every day and night.
Jesus is with them; they shine like a light.

LC3 takes great care of you and me.
Nate & Angela are great company.

LC3 loves God and they love people,
Although the Church does not have a steeple.

Nate & Angela George are man and wife.
We're here tonight to celebrate their life.

There is much more to say, but I'll be brief.
I try to provide some comic relief.

Season of Birth: Decatur Staleys 1920

There were 14 member teams of the American Professional Football Association (APFA) in 1920. [10] It was entirely possible for the two top teams to finish the season without a single common opponent. The teams were also scheduling games outside the league to teams that ran the gamut in quality from poor to highly competitive.

All of the Staleys in 1920 were considered rookies because it was the first year of play in the APFA. [11] The three most senior men on the team were 28 years old. Guy Chamberlin, at the age of 26, was a year older than his boss, player-coach George Halas. Chamberlin played left end and Halas played right end.

Loaded with talent, in addition to Halas and Chamberlin, the Staleys featured Hall of Famer George Trafton, Jimmy Conzelman, Halas's future Bears' partner Dutch Sternaman, and others. By most accounts, players in those days were very rugged men. Trafton was one of the biggest and roughest at 6-foot-2 and 230 pounds. He was known around the league for his aggressive style of play. According to Trafton's Pro Football Hall of Fame biography:

---

[10] This season description was originally printed in Patrick McCaskey's *Pillars of the NFL: Coaches Who Won Three or More Championships* published by Sporting Chance Press.

[11] It can be argued that there were professional football teams operating before 1920, but this year is generally considered the start of professional football because of the national scope of the league, the staying power and growth from this point forward, and the need to set a clear line of demarcation.

"Trafton was strongly disliked in every NFL city, with the exception of Green Bay and Rock Island. In those places, he was hated."[12]

Conzelman was a versatile back who would go on to win two NFL Championships as a head coach. The Staleys brought great excitement to Decatur and the Staley Starch Company. The team looked like a College All-Star team that could compete with any team in the country.

In the first two games of the season, the Staleys blew away two industrial teams, the Moline Universal Tractors, 20–0, and the Kewanee Walworths, 25–7. In the first match against a league rival, the Staleys traveled to Rock Island and beat the tough Independents, 7–0. Traveling to their future Chicago home, the Staleys shut out the Chicago Tigers, 10–0, at Cubs Park.[13] After beating Rockford A.C., 29–0, they played the Rock Island Independents again, but this time the game ended in a 0–0 tie. The media lauded the excellent wing play of the Staleys, that of Halas and Chamberlin. Also praised was Chamberlin's high knee action that makes him a terror to all opponents.[14]

The Minneapolis Marines gave the Staleys a tough game, but the Staleys prevailed, 3–0. The Staleys beat the Hammond Pros, 28–7, and once again shut out the Chicago Tigers, 6–0. Back to back battles against Paddy Driscoll's Chicago Cardinals pinned a 7–6 loss

---

[12] Pro Football hall of Fame Biography at
http://www.profootballhof.com/hof/member.aspx?PLAYER_ID=215 viewed on April 7, 2013.

[13] Cubs Park was renamed Wrigley Field in 1926.

[14] Wally Provost, "Chamberlin Missed Call on Pro Grid Growth," *Omaha World Herald*, September 5, 1964. (Provost quotes Chicago Daily News "terror to all" moniker for Chamberlin.)

on the Staley's pristine record, but the Staleys regrouped for another win, 10–0.

Hall of Famer Paddy Driscoll, who was a player-coach for the Cardinals, joined the Staleys for one game at the end of the season against the Akron Pros in what was billed the league championship.[15] The game featured the two best teams in the league, but a true championship game would not be built into the schedule for over a decade. The Akron Pros and the Decatur Staleys fought to a 0–0 tie.

The Staleys scored 164 points and allowed just 21 points from their opponents in 1920. They had a brilliant 10–1–2 season, but the Akron Pros finished with an 8–0–3 record. In the early days of the league, the champion was typically announced at the team owners' annual meeting and decided upon strictly by winning percentage with ties having no bearing. But by having the team owners make the decision after the season, arguments could at least be made. There were no playoffs, but there were disputes about who was truly deserving the top honor until the playoff system was introduced.

The Akron Pros had an awesome defense that year and scored 151 points while allowing just 7 from their opponents in their entire 11-game season. One notable contributor to the Akron championship run was Fritz Pollard, an African American running back and Hall of Famer. On April 30, 1921, when the team managers got together long after the season had ended, they voted Akron the league champion and gave them a loving cup

---

[15] Official web site of the Chicago Bears, Tradition Page at http://www.chicagobears.com/tradition/bears-in-the-hall/paddy-driscoll.html

that had been provided by the Brunswick-Balke Collender Company.[16]

In 1922, the owners would change the name of the league from the American Professional Football Association (APFA) to the National Football League (NFL) at the urging of George Halas.

Joe Stydahar and Birth of the Draft

"Jumbo Joe" Stydahar was born in Kaylor, Pennsylvania. He attended Shinnston High School in Shinnston, West Virginia. He played college football for the West Virginia Mountaineers. Stydahar was the first player ever drafted by the Chicago Bears in the inaugural draft of 1936. The Hall of Fame tackle was 6-foot-4 and 245 pounds. Halas considered him a man of great character who "knew what was good and right in life." He played for 7 years for the Bears (1936-1942) then served in the Navy during World War II for 2 years. He returned to the Bears (1945-1946) for another 2 more years. Stydahar was a 4-time All Pro and was a 4-time NFL Pro Bowler. He played on the Chicago Bears Championship teams of 1940, 1941, and 1946. Like many Bears of his day, he was the ultimate tough guy on the field and a conscientious citizen off the field.

Stydahar was named one of the Top 100 Bears of All Time. He was inducted into the Pro Football Hall of fame Class of 1967.

---

[16] Bob Carroll, Akron Pros 1920, *The Coffin Corner*: Vol. 4, No. 12 (1982), viewed at http://www.profootballresearchers.org/Coffin_Corner/04-12-119.pdf on April 3, 2013.

Bill Hewitt

Bill Hewitt was born in Bay City Michigan and attended Bay City Central High School. In college, he played for the University of Michigan at both fullback and end. As a pro, Hewitt played for the Chicago Bears for his first 5 seasons (1932-1936) and then finished out his career with 3 more seasons in Philadelphia. He retired in 1939 and then came back in 1943 to play for the Steagles (a combined WWII team of the Eagles and Steelers that enabled both teams to continue during a financial crisis for the NFL).

Several retired players like Hewitt returned from retirement during the war.

In Chicago, Hewitt had 52 receptions for 939 yards and 19 touchdowns. The passing game was much more modest in Hewitt's era. In 1934, he was the league leader in touchdown receptions with 5. Overall for his career, he had 103 receptions for 1,638 yards and 23 touchdowns.

Hewitt was exceptional on both offense and defense. On defense he seemed to have a second sense for exactly when the ball was centered—he was nicknamed the "Offside Kid" because opposing teams thought he was offside. In response, Hewitt would point out that the refs were watching carefully and they didn't see it that way! On offense in critical situations, Hewitt especially enjoyed trick plays that fooled unsuspecting defenders. He was said to be the creator of some of those schemes. He was a 4-time All Pro. Hewitt was enshrined into the Pro Football Hall of Fame Class of 1971. He was named as one of the Top 100 Bears of All Time.

Danny Fortmann

Many Chicago Bears players made tremendous contributions to football and society. Danny Fortmann was one of those. Fortmann was born in Pearl River, New York, and he attended Pearl River High School. No slouch, he played many sports in high school. He was his class's valedictorian. He attended Colgate University and played guard there where he also excelled scholastically.

The Bears' 9th pick in the first draft in 1936, Fortmann attended the University of Chicago Medical School while in his early pro seasons and then practiced medicine in his later ones. He played from 1936-1943. He was a solid leader on the Bears 1940, 1941, and 1943 Championship teams.

Fortmann received high marks for his work on the offensive line where he was a proficient blocker. On defense, his intelligence came through as he was renowned for his ability to diagnose plays. At 6-foot and 210 pounds, he was small but determined. An All Pro five times, he was invited to the Pro Bowl in three seasons. He lived a full life practicing medicine at the highest level and helping out in sports for various organizations. He was a life-long loyal friend of "Papa Bear" George Halas.

Fortmann served in the Navy during World War II as a medical doctor. Fortmann was inducted into the Pro Football Hall of Fame Class of 1965. He was named one of the Top 100 Bears of All Time.

LOST AND FOUND

In relation
To the parable
Of the prodigal son,
I have been the younger son.
I have been rebellious.
I have been the older son.
I have been resentful.
Now my goal is to be the father.
Forgive others as I have been forgiven

—PKPMc

The Prodigal Son learns some great lessons and returns to the father who loves him. At times we are lost sheep and then we are found.

John Madden

On April 10, 1936, John Madden was born in Austin, Minnesota, home of Hormel Foods and the Spam Museum. His father, Earl Russell Madden, was an auto mechanic. His mother was Mary Margaret Madden. When Madden was beginning school age, the family moved to Daly, California, just south of San Francisco. Madden attended Our Lady of Perpetual Help Grade School. He played football at Jefferson High School and graduated in 1954.

Madden had one of those complicated California College careers that you need a scorecard to track. He was a lineman and would play mostly at offensive tackle, but he could play defense as well. He played at the

College of San Mateo for one year and then he was given a scholarship to the University of Oregon. A knee injury and surgery halted his play there. He decided to leave Oregon and he transferred to Grays Harbor College in Aberdeen, Washington, in 1956 where he played for the Chokers. Finally, he found a home at Cal Poly in San Luis Obispo where he played football in 1957 and 1958. At San Luis Obispo, he also earned a Bachelors and Masters in Education. He married his girlfriend, Virginia, in 1959.

Don't Worry About the Horse Being Blind, Just Load the Wagon[17]

Madden was drafted in 1958 by the Philadelphia Eagles, but another knee injury ended his football dream before his pro career could get started. But Madden wasted no time. He didn't worry about what he could not control. He moved into coaching. He became an avid student of the game. His coaching career progressed quickly. After coaching at a community college called Allan Hancock College in Santa Maria from 1960-1963, he moved on to San Diego State in 1964, where he was an assistant coach under Don "Air" Coryell through 1966. In 1967, he became an assistant coach for the Oakland Raiders and in 1969 at age 32, he took over as head coach.

Madden was a lively and demonstrative coach on the sidelines. Oakland players were from many different backgrounds. Madden handled his personnel well by keeping things simple with his rules. In turn, he was well respected by his players. He was also a winner.

---

[17] A saying Madden used at many halftimes when coaching. He said it fired up his players though he did not understand it. Another version is "Don't worry about the mule, just load the wagons." It means do what you can do and don't worry about what is out of your control.

In his 10-year head-coaching career, Madden was 103–32–7 with a .759 winning percentage. He coached the 1976 Raiders to a Super Bowl XI victory, 32–14, over the Vikings at the Rose Bowl. Madden was inducted into the Pro Football Hall of Fame in 2006.

Madden had an abhorrence of flying. At the end of his coaching career it became debilitating. Madden surprised many observers when he retired from coaching at age 42 saying that he had nothing left to give. He was not well and looking forward to spending more time with his wife Virginia, and sons, Joseph and Michael. He would later say that he found that his family had their own lives to live. He joked that he was spending a lot of time with the family dog.[18] He started announcing football games. Madden's knowledge of the game, his enthusiasm for it, and his colloquial way of describing it, made him a rising star. Madden had a great deal of respect for the game, but at the same time, he never took himself too seriously behind the microphone.

Madden would make alternative travel plans to avoid plane travel. His popular appeal with sponsors generated perks on the train and later private bus travel. Madden's travels across America on assignment gave him a kind of Charles Kuralt "On the Road" and John Steinbeck *Travels with Charley* persona.[19] Stops along the way to diners and shops would be enthusiastically greeted by average Americans. Photos with Madden and

---

[18] See ESPN Podcast, *Madden's Game*, for a comprehensive story on the development and players at https://30for30podcasts.com/episodes/maddens-game/ .

[19] Scott Oustler, "John Madden's cruise through life was a joy for him, and for us," *San Francisco Chronicle*, December 29, 2021, viewed at https://www.msn.com/en-us/sports/nfl/john-madden-s-cruise-through-life-was-a-joy-for-him-and-for-us/ar-AASfRnV on December 20, 2021.

personal conversations with the coach would be cherished.

He worked with CBS from 1979 through 1993, often teaming up with Pat Summerall.[20] Madden and Summerall joined Fox's NFL coverage after the network gained the rights to broadcast NFC games from 1994 through 2001. In 2002, Madden became a commentator on ABC's Monday Night Football with play-by-play announcer Al Michaels. Beginning with the 2006 season, Madden provided color commentary for NBC's Sunday night NFL games. He continued at NBC until his retirement following his work on Super Bowl XLIII on February 1, 2009, between the Arizona Cardinals and the Pittsburgh Steelers.

Madden Video Game

Madden was asked by Trip Hawkins, who studied computers and game theory at Harvard University, to help him develop a realistic football video game for Electronic Arts. Madden worked with developers, provided a playbook and insisted that they understood his vision for such a product. He wanted the game to provide a learning experience for game players and to be authentic. With Madden on board, the game development was likely slowed because of this vision. The development team made it through some rough years before the first version of "John Madden Football" was launched in 1988. Then technology improved and video games became more captivating as competition increased in the marketplace. NFL endorsement was solicited and obtained. Under its new name, "Madden NFL" became an even greater

---

[20] Both John Madden and Pat Summerall were inducted into the Sports Broadcasting Hall of Fame in 2010.

blockbuster video game franchise that achieved popularity with football gamers who included many NFL players and even coaches. The Madden-game world became a kind of parallel universe to professional football. The realistic game played out in a superb video venue that had been anything but realistic to start. At the same time, back in the real-world NFL, television would be influenced by video games.

The popularity of the Madden video game was not lost on David Hill when he was hired to be president of Fox Sports.[21] Hill loved the video game experience and wanted to add some of its elements to the TV coverage. One of the things that Fox did was use special equipment that helped capture authentic sounds of the game and bring them into the living room, just as they had been present in the video game. From the quarterback shouting out signals to the crash of pads when players collide, these elements were captured and delivered with new clarity to the TV audience. Video game inspired enhancements continue to this day with more creative graphic images at the start of games, wide screens in stadiums, spectacular lighting arrangements and more.

Madden's involvement in Madden NFL continued in some capacity until his death. Madden was a stickler for realism and this contributed to constant development and improvements making Madden a household name.

John Madden died on December 28, 2021. On Christmas Day, December 25, 2021, the Fox network presented "All Madden," a documentary on Madden's tremendous coaching and broadcasting career.

---

[21] See ESPN Podcast, *Madden's Game,* for a comprehensive story on the development and players at
https://30for30podcasts.com/episodes/maddens-game/ .

Madden's Contributions to the Game

Madden was an enthusiastic supporter of professional football. Madden was one of the most prominent and influential persons in NFL football as a splendid coach, an honest and entertaining broadcaster, and a football video game developer who insisted on integrity. Madden kept everything real for those around him, but he always did it with enthusiasm.

Sid Caesar, John Belushi, and an Excellent Question

A generation separated Sid Caesar and John Belushi, but they shared much in common. Caesar was an early TV comedy pioneer, one of the most-recognized Americans in the 1950s. Belushi rocketed to fame in the 1970s on Saturday Night Live.[22] Both were loved by millions of fans. Both fought off personal demons that often come with a quick rise to celebrity and wealth. Caesar survived his problems and lived to be 91. Belushi died at age 33.

In 1982, John Callaway interviewed Sid Caesar for the Chicago Tonight Program. That show was posted online on February 13, 2014, the day after Caesar's death. Late in the interview, John Callaway asked Sid Caesar, "If you could have talked to John Belushi before he died, what would you have said to John Belushi if you had known the problems that he had? Is there anything you can say?"

Sid Caesar replied, "I don't know if he would have listened. Hey, easy does it. Don't try to swallow the whole world in one gulp. And look at yourself.

---

[22] In 2015, *Rolling Stone* magazine ranked John Belushi as the top Saturday Night Live cast member of all time.

Appreciate life. You don't have to have all this circus going on around you. Stop and smell the roses. Listen to the birds. All the clichés are true. That's why they're clichés because you've heard them a million times. Because they're true. Stop. If your life is that hectic, hold it. It's not worth it. It really isn't. Success is in your own head. If you think you're successful, I don't care if you just come in a door and say hi, you did it right. That's a success."[23]

Ken Geiger

I was privileged to know Ken Geiger. He had a long industrious life. People of all ages who knew Geiger often remembered his positive influence on their lives.

On December 30, 1931, Geiger was born in Berwyn, Illinois. He went to Saint Leonard's School. He played football and boxed for Fenwick High School in Oak Park. He played football and baseball for Monmouth College.

After Geiger had served in the Army, he earned a master's degree at the University of Illinois and coached the freshmen offensive linemen. He earned a Doctorate in Education at the University of Missouri and was the assistant varsity line coach. Then he returned to Monmouth College as varsity line coach.

For 34 years, Geiger taught and coached at Morton High Schools interscholastic program. He was head football coach, wrestling coach, athletic director, and department chair. Many of the young men whom he had coached continued to call him Coach until he died.

Geiger worked for the Chicago Bears for 11 years, the Indianapolis Colts for 5 years, and the New Orleans

---

[23] See interview on YouTube, viewed at https://www.youtube.com/watch?v=r_HolCj1ACs on November 16, 2021.

Saints for 3 years. Then he helped bring American football to Europe.

When Geiger worked for the Bears, he arranged for the team to have cold weather practices in the Morton High School Fieldhouse. He and his wife, Sheryl, attended the Bears' victory in Super Bowl XX. When Mike Ditka had a heart attack at Halas Hall; Geiger stayed with him until the paramedics arrived.

Geiger is in the Monmouth College Hall of Fame. He is in the Chicago Catholic League Hall of Fame.

Geiger and his wife, Sheryl, were married for 67 years. They lived in the same house in which he grew up in Berwyn. They had five children, three grandchildren, and three great-grandchildren. He died, at the age of 89, on January 21, 2021. The Funeral was at Saint Leonard's Church on January 27.

Geiger was a lifelong parishioner at Saint Leonard's. In the beginning, he sat in the back of the Church so that he could tell jokes and stories. At the end, he sat in the front of the Church so that he could be closer to the Lord.

Learning from Father Sparough and Father Rossman

Bellarmine Jesuit Retreat House is located on 80 acres 40 miles northwest of Chicago. The Bellarmine grounds are described on their website as a peaceful setting for reflection and spiritual contemplation. Indoors, the chapels, conference center, lounges, library, and individual private rooms maintain a comfortable and tranquil environment for retreatants.[24]

From Friday, February 7, through Sunday, February 9, 2020, Father Michael Sparough, S.J. and Father Michael Rossman, S.J., gave a series of eight talks on the Our Father at Bellarmine Jesuit Retreat House.

Here are ten thoughts from the talks that I want to share with you:

1. *God is as close to us as our own family members.*
2. *We are children of the same Father. We are called to overcome division.*
3. *Praise God for being God. He wants us to be the best version of ourselves.*
4. *God loves us individually. He looks us in the eye. Let's be open to His encouragement.*
5. *God gives us serenity and strength to give up addictions one day at a time.*
6. *We are in no position to receive God's mercy unless we forgive others. Forgive others and receive God's mercy.*
7. *Repentance leads to the abundance that God can give us. Repentance is the beginning of hope.*
8. *Gratitude makes us joyful.*
9. *God wants us to succeed*
10. *Come with a humble heart before God.*

Linebacker Urlacher and Safety Brown

On April 15, 2000, the Bears drafted Brian Urlacher in the first round and Mike Brown in the second.

---

[24] See the Retreat Center's website at
https://jesuitsmidwest.org/Retreat-Center-Detail?TN=CODE-20130409084923

Two players, both alike in dignity,
In fair Chicago, where we play our games.

When Brian wore the orange and blue,
He excelled in cover two.
He filled gaps and made tackles.
He forced fumbles and sacked quarterbacks.
He made key interceptions.

It seems like twelve years,
Since Mike played for the Bears.
He tackled and he intercepted.
When he was here,
We were at full strength.

Devin Hester

NFL teams are always looking for a new unexpected advantage against competition. There was no better such advantage than Devin Hester. For football fans, he made every game more interesting. For his opponents, if they lost focus on Hester for half a second on a kickoff or a punt return, he would not be found until the end zone.

Hester was a second round draft pick for the Bears in 2006. From his first year on the Bears roster, he excelled at kickoff and punt returns. He was a huge factor on the Bears journey to the Super Bowl. In Super Bowl XLI against the Indianapolis Colts, Hester ran the opening kickoff back 92 yards for a touchdown in the first seconds of the game. The Colts managed to keep the ball away from Hester for the remainder of the game and won, 29-17.

Watching the highlight films of Hester's returns for touchdowns, speed was always a key factor and he accelerated in split seconds. He had a subtlety in his moves which allowed him to avoid wasted motion. He made small adjustments in direction even before he caught the ball. He was able to make quick changes as well, but it was usually about speed. On some of his touchdown runs, he was hardly touched.

Hester was magic on the football field. His role would eventually include wide receiver as the Bears tried to get him more playing time. Hester would play 8 years for the Bears and finish out his career with the Atlanta Falcons and the Baltimore Ravens plus a final playoff run with the Seattle Seahawks.

For the Bears, Hester returned 264 punts for 3,241 yards and 13 touchdowns. He returned 222 kickoffs for 5,504 yards for 5 touchdowns. As a Bear receiver, he had 217 receptions for 2,807 yards and 14 touchdowns. He was a 3-time All Pro and invited to the Pro Bowl four times. He led the league in punt-return yards in 2006 and 2010, and kick-return yards in 2013 and 2014. He holds several records for returners.

Hester is remembered by football fans as one of the most exciting players in the history of the game and the greatest return man of all-time. He was named one of the Top 100 Bears of All Time.

Lucky Luis Lesmond

On Saturday, February 20, 2021, the Notre Dame College Prep varsity basketball team played at Fenwick. At the end of overtime, Louis Lesmond of Notre Dame made a half-court shot to win the game. In commemoration of the event, I have written "Louie Lesmond," a poem to commemorate the occasion.

Louie Lesmond

From home to home, we all can roam and read a poem
to one
From Notre Dame
Who won the game.
He came to us from France just like the C.S.C.
Catholic school
Is really cool!

Louie Lesmond! Made a great shot
After the game, thank him a lot.
Classmates, teammates—he knows them all
The kind of a Don who is walking quite tall!
Louie Lesmond! Great team player
In the gym a dragon slayer,
Louie Lesmond helped the game
And his teammates feel the same.

He is a Don, a gentleman who helped us win with joy
Notre Dame lad!
The school is glad!
Everywhere we pray for him to handle all the fame
He made the shot
For victory!

Our Friends at MK Spices

In 1922, M. K. Summers started Marion-Kay Spices in
Springfield, Missouri. Then they moved to Saint Louis.
In 1949, they moved to Brownstown, Indiana.
Summers's daughter, Madelyn, and her husband, Jim
Reid, were the next generation owners. Three of their
children, Pamela Warren, Kordell Reid, and Kathy
Meador, are extending the family legacy.

I have known the family since 1974. My wife, Gretchen, uses their spices at home. In honor of the MK Spices, I have written this poem.

MK Spices

We want to cook
With MK Spices
We could eat quite well
The rest of our lives
With MK Spices

Family pictures
On company walls
You see us together
We answer your calls
MK Spices

One hundred years
Of spices for you
We lead the cheers
And we don't talk blue
MK Spices

You buy spices now
We will make it somehow
We need another chance
All of your food we will enhance
Yours in good taste

Julius Peppers

Julius Peppers is an extraordinary athlete in an age of great talent. Talent is best measured in performance. Peppers played in both the NFL Super Bowl and the

NCAA Final Four.[25] Growing up in Bailey, North Carolina, Peppers attended Southern Nash High School and then went on to the University of North Carolina, which is known for its tremendous basketball program. At 6-foot-7, 295 pounds, Peppers was suited for both football and basketball.

Peppers played football at North Carolina from 1999-2001. He was a disruptive defensive player, a first-team All American in 2001. He won the Chuck Bednarik Award as the nation's top defensive player along with the Lombardi Award given to the nation's top college lineman.

Named after basketball star Julius Irving, Peppers also hoped to contribute in basketball. It turned out he was a godsend for Basketball Head Coach Bill Guthridge who had lost several players to injuries. Peppers came off the bench to not just fill-in, but he helped keep the team alive in the playoffs. The Tar Heels played in the 2000 Final Four. Their season ended when they lost, 71-59, to Florida in the NCAA tournament national semifinals.

Peppers was selected in the first round of the 2002 draft by the Carolina Panthers. He was the Defensive Rookie of the Year. He was defensive end for the Panthers from 2002-2009 and then came back to Carolina for his last two seasons in 2017-2018. He played in Super Bowl XXXVIII, February 1, 2004, for Panthers Head Coach John Fox when the New England Patriots beat the Panthers in a tight game, 32-29. He played for the Bears from 2010-2013, from age 30-33. Peppers had incredible size, speed, and endurance. For the Bears he had 37.5 sacks and 175 tackles. Like some of the best defensive ends, Peppers was frequently double-teamed.

---

[25] Scott Fowler, *North Carolina Tar Heels: Where Have You Gone?* (Champaign, IL: Sports Publishing LLC, 2005) 171.

His teammates were big fans. Peppers went on to play outside linebacker for the Green Bay Packers for three seasons from 2014-2016 before heading back to Carolina.

Overall, Peppers had 159.5 sacks and 719 tackles in 17 seasons. He was an All Pro for three seasons and invited to the Pro Bowl nine times. Peppers was a force for the Bears and was named one of the Top 100 Bears of All Time.

My Complete Baseball Knowledge

Fielders, stay down on ground balls.
Hitters, hit line drives in the gaps.
Pitchers, throw strikes, most of the time.

Double plays help the pitch count.
When there are runners on base,
A strike out prevents the runners from advancing.

Gale Sayers Speaks to Troops

GIVING

"This is the beginning of a new day. God has given me this day to use as I will. I can waste it or use it for good, but what I do today is important, because I am exchanging a day of my life for it! When tomorrow comes, this day will be gone forever, leaving in its place something that I have traded for it. I want it to be gain, and not loss; good, and not evil; success, and not failure; in order that I shall not regret the price I have paid for it."

—Heartsill Wilson[26]

We commit ourselves to our faith and our fellow man. We come together to do great things that are impossible to accomplish by ourselves. We give and we learn each day.

Humble Priest Beatified

Bernard Francis Casey was born of Irish immigrant parents in 1870 in a cabin on a farm near Prescott, Wisconsin. The farm was a humble homestead in the northwest portion of the state near the Mississippi River and the Minnesota border. Casey was the sixth child of 16: 10 boys and six girls. In his youth, Casey and his brothers enjoyed playing baseball. Bernard was catcher. Not surprising, he has a special place of reverence to many in the baseball community.

---

[26] This poem has often been attributed to "anonymous," but recently some sites suggest it was written by automobile executive and motivational speaker Heartsill Wilson who died in 1994. The likes of Bear Bryant and many others were known to carry the poem around with them or have it typed up on a sheet of paper to read every day. See https://www.findagrave.com/memorial/208484751/heartsill-wilson .

As a young boy, Casey contracted diphtheria, a life-threatening infection caused by strains of bacteria that commonly infect the respiratory system. Casey survived, but two of his siblings did not. Casey's voice was impaired by the disease.

As a young adult, the industrious Casey worked as a logger, a hospital orderly, a prison guard, and a street car operator to help his large family. At age 21, he entered Saint Francis High School Seminary, a German speaking school in suburban Milwaukee to study for the diocesan priesthood. Language troubles led him to leave the diocesan seminary and enter a religious order, the Capuchins in Detroit in 1897, where he received his religious name of Solanus. The Capuchins were also German-speaking. More language difficulties led his superiors to allow him to be ordained with certain conditions as a "simplex" priest. They did not believe he was capable to preach and hear confessions. Ordained in 1904, the humble Father Solanus spent his first 20 years in New York City and another 20 years at Saint Bonaventure Monastery in Detroit. In 1945, he returned to New York for a year at Saint Michael's in Brooklyn, then he moved on to Huntington, Indiana, from 1946 to 1956. He was reassigned to Saint Bonaventure in the last year of his life in 1956.

Father Solanus spent a good part of his service as someone who opened the door to visitors and guests at the various monasteries where he lived, meeting many people in times of trouble who sought prayers and advice. In return, he encouraged people to improve their own spiritual lives and support the missions.

Father Solanus was also known to play the violin for his fellow monks.

Father Solanus had a particular love of the poor and troubled. Even without preaching homilies or hearing confessions, he was able to reach many wherever he was assigned. After his death, voluminous records of his work recorded in his own hand were found among his otherwise meagre possessions. Notations of the aid people received from his prayers and intercessions were sometimes noted. Many people credited his intercession with help in their lives and the Capuchins decided to begin work on the cause for sainthood. Father Solanus's influence was also evidenced by the 8,000 people who were present at his funeral.

Many have worked on the process of sainthood for Father Solanus. A biographical history of Father Solanus was submitted to the Congregation for Causes of Saints that in turn gave their recommendation to Pope John Paul II on July 11, 1995. His Holiness promulgated the Decree of Heroic Virtue giving Father Solanus Casey the title of "Venerable Solanus Casey." Postulators began gathering evidence of healings from the intercession of Father Solanus Casey. A first miraculous healing was investigated and approved by Pope Francis. Father Solanus is now Beatified and is now known as Blessed. He was proclaimed Blessed on November 18, 2017, in Ford Field in Detroit with 60,000 in attendance. Ford Field is the multi-purpose indoor stadium that is home of the Detroit Lions. One more miracle attributed to the intercession of the humble Capuchin is necessary in the Canonization process.

Dick Hoyt, John Kerry, Bryan Lyons, and Rick Hoyt

Dick and Rick Hoyt

It's hard to put words into what father and son, Dick and Rick Hoyt have given each other. Maybe you have seen the many inspirational videos and news stories on the Hoyts.[27] Dick brought his son Rick who has cerebral palsy with him when competing as Team Hoyt in marathons, triathlons, and even Iron Man contests. It was Rick's expression of pleasure after they finished a 5-mile charity run that started their careers in endurance sport. After that first experience, Rick told his dad that when they were in the race, it felt like his disability had disappeared. Dick did everything possible to provide the experience over and over again competing in hundreds of triathlons, over 30 Boston Marathons, and many other events. Rick was an inspiration to his dad and that inspiration kept him competing until his mid-70s.

Dick pushed his son Rick (in running events), pulled Rick (in water events in a raft), and rode with him (in biking events) over hundreds of finish lines. Oh, and they also ran and biked across the country! The Hoyts have achieved some remarkable performances as a team, but perhaps more important than their sports accomplishments is how powerfully their story has affected others for the good.

Many honors have been presented to the Hoyts over the years. Perhaps the most noteworthy is a bronze statue depicting the Hoyts in competition that was installed a few yards from the Boston Marathon starting line.

Created in 1989, the Hoyt Foundation "aspires to build the individual character, self-confidence and self-

---

[27] There are many video stories on Dick and Rick Hoyt, here is one: https://www.youtube.com/watch?v=oYUhGMugpM8

esteem of America's disabled young people through inclusion in all facets of daily life; including family and community activities, especially sports, at home, in schools, and in the workplace."

Dick Hoyt, who inspired thousands of runners, fathers and disabled athletes by competing with his son, Rick, died March 17, 2021. He was 80. Bryan Lyons, a member of Team Hoyt, who pushed Rick in recent years, passed away at age 50 in 2020.

Gale Sayers

Gale Sayers was a remarkable player. Exceptionally elusive, he used every inch of his body to twist and turn through defensive lines and past their best players. Sayers could see or sense everyone around him on the field. Once beyond the line of scrimmage, he could accelerate through almost any size hole to daylight. And his moves seemed perfectly choreographed for the budding television audience—reels of highlight films followed him. His career was short—five productive seasons and two cut short with injuries and rehab.

In 1968, Sayers had a devastating injury to his right knee. Teammate Brian Piccolo encouraged Sayers through successful rehabilitation. In 1969, Sayers led the league in rushing. That same year, the 26-year old Piccolo was afflicted with terminal cancer.

Sayers received the George Halas Award for Courage for his comeback. He accepted the award shortly before Piccolo's death in 1970.

Sadly, injury to Sayers's left knee followed in 1970 and he struggled to recover, but could not.

Sayers was a 5-time All Pro and was named to 4 Pro Bowls. Sayers was named to the Pro Football Hall of Fame All-1960s Team and the NFL 100 All-Time Team.

In 1977, my grandfather, George Halas, presented Sayers for induction into the Pro Football Hall of Fame. Recognizing the significance of the occasion, my father served as speechwriter.

"Today I tell you that if you would see perfection at running back you had best get a film of Gale Sayers. He was poetry in motion and we shall never see his like again."

Sayers went on to a successful career in sports administration and business. On September 23, 2020, he passed away at age 77.

Bears Who Care

Many Bears practice good works. Bears do care! Here's a poem about two.

Jay Cutler and Tommie Harris

On April twenty-nine, nineteen eighty-three,
Jay Cutler and Tommie Harris were born
In different hospitals. So, there's no way
Their parents brought home the wrong babies.

Jay had a cannon arm and quick release.
He set many Bears' passing records.
He was at his best when he accepted
The Piccolo Award for Josh McCown.

Tommie's a singer; he doesn't do blue.
His father's a preacher; Tommie is too.
Tommie was great with the eight-step handshake.
He is terrific; he is not a fake.

Tommie was at his best when he preached
At Lawndale Community Church.

Tommie Harris Signs Autograph for Sr. Master Sgt. Marc Pumala

Tommie Harris

Tommie Harris was born in Germany and raised in Killeen, Texas. He went to Ellison High School and then enrolled at the University of Oklahoma. He played for Bob Stoops Sooners where he won the Lombardi Award for the Nation's best lineman in 2003. Stoops said he "almost" felt sorry for opponents because Harris was "impossible to block."

Harris who at 6-foot-3, 295 pounds was a first-round draft choice of the Chicago Bears and Head Coach Lovie Smith in 2004. Harris played defensive tackle for the Bears from 2004-2010 and then he played one season for the San Diego Chargers. His Bears career was strong in the first several seasons and then slowed due to injuries. He was a Pro Bowler in 2005, 2006, and 2007.

The 2006 Bears defense took them into the playoffs right up to Super Bowl XLI against the Indianapolis Colts, which they lost 29-17 (without Harris, due to injury). Harris is one of the Top 100 Bears of All Time.

Jay Cutler

Jay Cutler was born in Santa Claus, Indiana, and played his high school ball at nearby Heritage Hills High School in Lincoln City. Cutler played basketball, baseball, and football in high school. From southern Indiana, he traveled 160 miles south to attend Vanderbilt University in Nashville. Cutler's football performance at Vanderbilt was exceptional, never missing a game once he was the starting quarterback, setting records in many categories, competing and beating teams the Commodores rarely played well, and being named the SEC Offensive Player of the Year in 2005.

Cutler had the strength, size, and intelligence to score almost every time he took the field. Drafted by the Denver Broncos in 2005, at 6-foot-3 and 230 pounds, Cutler looked strong and played well for the Broncos. In his third season with the Broncos, Cutler was a Pro-Bowl quarterback who passed for 4,526 yards, 25 touchdowns with 18 interceptions and suffered just 11 sacks.

Cutler was acquired by the Chicago Bears and played in Chicago from 2009-2016. In 2010, Cutler and the Bears would win the NFC North Division. In 8 seasons, Cutler would complete 2,020 passes for 23,443 yards, 154 touchdowns, 109 interceptions with a quarterback rating of 85.2. Cutler leads the Bears in completions, touchdowns, team record in games started, and comebacks led by a quarterback. Cutler is one of the Top

100 Bears of All Time named by respected journalists Don Pierson and Dan Pompei.

Fatima Movie

In Covid times, a friend of mine, Lisa Wheeler, asked me to introduce the new "Fatima" movie for the Daughters of Saint Paul at a special showing at Soldier Field. "Fatima" is about the Marian Apparitions and the little children who witnessed them in Portugal. Of the three little children to whom Mary appeared, Francisco and Jacinta Marto died just a few years after the apparitions from the Great Spanish Flu Epidemic. The third child, Lucia, became a nun and lived modestly in two different convents until the age of 97. In Sister Lucia's portrayal in the movie as an elderly nun, she is asked if she has any regrets. Without any hint of self-importance, Sister Lucia states that she wished she would have done better in getting our Lady's message across to the world.

My Introduction

Hello. My name is Pat McCaskey. I'm at home now so this is a recording.

I am not a daughter of Saint Paul, but my Confirmation name is Paul. He wrote a lot of letters even though the Corinthians were the only ones who ever wrote back. Wherever he spoke there was either a revival or a riot.

When I was a student at Saint Mary's School in Des Plaines, we saw many wonderful movies in the school hall for ten cents that went to the missions. We saw "The Bells of Saint Mary's" "The Glenn Miller Story," "The Pride of the Yankees," "The Spirit of Saint Louis," and "The Student Prince."

TUITION REBATE

Tonight, we get to see the movie "Fatima." We serve a mighty God. You might be asking why I am doing a welcome video. Lisa Wheeler contacted me much as Our Lady appeared to the three children of Fatima.

Fatima draws thousands of pilgrims from around the world with its night-time processions. Pilgrims come to the Cova de Iria where the Virgin Mary appeared. On one side of the plaza rises the great basilica housing the tombs of Saint Francisco and Saint Jacinta Marto. Today the principal pilgrimage festivals take place on the anniversaries of the original appearances.

Thank you for listening. This is better than talking to myself. It is great to be with you. Have a Hall of Fame night.

Why a New Movie on Fatima?

Sr. Nancy Usselmann of the Daughters of Saint Paul reviewed the new movie, "Fatima." She explains that "The Miracle of Our Lady of Fatima" (1952) produced by Warner Bros. and directed by John Brahm was the first major motion picture about the miraculous events of Fatima.

This old Warner Bros. film was well received by viewers. So the key question is: Why do we need another movie on Fatima? Well it's all about reaching a new audience and creating some excitement over something new. Young people will more likely see something new than seek out old films from half a century ago!

Fatima Story

In the spring and summer of 1916, 9-year-old Lúcia Santos and her cousins, Jacinta and Francisco Marto, were herding sheep at the Cova da Iria near their home village of Fátima. They were visited by an angel who taught them prayers and encouraged sacrifice. The angel appeared two more times. The following year, on May 13, 1917, Lúcia described seeing a lady "brighter than the sun..." Jacinta told her family about the apparition. Her mother told neighbors and they spread the news. Appearances on June 13 and July 13 occurred in which the lady asked the children to do penance and acts of reparation and make personal sacrifices to save sinners. Lúcia recounted that the lady gave the children three secrets, which have intrigued the public since.

Thousands of people came to Fátima to see the apparitions. On August 13, 1917, a local politician, Artur Santos, intercepted and jailed the children before they could reach the Cova da Iria. He threatened the children because they were causing a commotion. The children had their next apparition on August 15, the Feast of the Assumption, at nearby Valinhos. On October 13, 1917, what became known as the "Miracle of the Sun" occurred at Fatima. At Cova da Iria, a huge crowd stood with the children. Lúcia, seeing light rising from the lady's hands and the sun appearing as a silver disk, called out "look at the sun" as it changed colors and rotated. The children saw various images of Our Lady and the Holy Family that day.

In October 1930, after a canonical inquiry, the apparitions of Fátima were said to be "worthy of belief." Popes Pius XII (1939-1958), John XXIII (1958-1963), Paul VI (1963-1978), John Paul II (1978-2005), Benedict XVI (2005-2013), and Francis (2013-) have all supported the Fátima events. Most notably, Pope Saint John Paul II credited the intercession of Our Lady of Fatima for saving his life following an assassination attempt on the Feast of Our Lady of Fatima in 1981. The bullet from his wound was placed in the crown of the Virgin's statue.

Patrick McCaskey at WSFI Radio Studio

Patrick McCaskey

EXPRESSING

Isaiah the Prophet was a writer.
Who was smart enough to let God use him.
—PKPMc

What follows a long education is more education. Even when we put our education to work in expressing our thoughts, we are still learning.

Pandemic Moats Lead to Quarantine Notes

Jesus Christ was an excellent lector.
He stuck to the text. He did not ad lib.

I agree with Anthony Esolen.[28]
"There is no Easter without Good Friday."
I am not a Doctor of the Church,
But I do have lifesaving merit badge.

Meekness is not weakness; it defeats wrath.
Fervor defeats sloth; rock breaks scissors.
Scissors cut paper; paper covers rock.

It's important to develop four ways.
Physically, I have recess daily.
Socially, I keep distance readily.
Culturally, I'm reading and writing.
Spiritually, "Divine Comedy."

---

[28] Anthony Esolen is a professor and writer in residence at Magdalen College of the Liberal Arts, in Warner, New Hampshire.

My Poetry

Poetry is literary work that is an intense expression of feelings and ideas. Ideas are powerful. In Illinois, we are lucky to have Abraham Lincoln as our patron of thought. Carl Sandburg reinforced that. While the literary world can often look at cracks in our foundation, my writing has often been about promoting the good. And I think we need more of that today.

Return to Indiana University

On Monday, February 10, 2020, I returned to Indiana University as a luminary, a distinguished alumnus. My first stop was Alpha Epsilon Phi sorority where I had lived during my last two semesters as the houseboy for seventy ladies. While I was living there, I took Recent Hebrew Literature courses. Leah Goldberg's poem "Remembrance of Beginnings of Things" left an impression on me. After dinner, I read that poem to the current ladies.

Among many activities the next day, I met with my friend and former teacher, Distinguished Professor Emeritus Scott Russell Sanders in the Eskenazi Museum of Art. I visited a class: The Craft of Poetry in Lindley Hall with Professor Catherine Bowman.

Before the pandemic, I was speaking at over 100 engagements a year, no fee for me. These speeches often included reading essays and poems.

I record essays and poems for broadcast on WSFI Radio, 88.5 FM. These are broadcast in northern Illinois and southern Wisconsin.

My Writing Roots

Over 150 years ago, my great-great grandfather, educator, and publisher J. P. McCaskey wrote: "I have to be in touch intellectually and spiritually with the best souls of the present and the past, with their strength and goodness..."

Writings that focus on good habits and life lessons are part of my experiences. Exceptional athletes have been a part of my life as have family friends who have devoted their lives to the poor and underserved. My writings often focus on these people. My program is a practical one that provides literature with a purpose; literature that is accessible; literature that includes humor; and literature that calls attention to some of the people who are or have been important including those from many cultures. I celebrate people who work for the common good.

The topic of sports is used as a metaphor for life lessons in literature, but it is more than that. Today most people understand that sports and fitness foster a better citizen, one who is healthier and a greater contributor to society. Sports are attention getting. I like poetry that includes sports as its theme.

More than anything else, I enjoy presenting work, meeting different audiences, and reading essays and poems to them.

Some of my recent speaking engagements have been virtual like the Notre Dame College Prep Gala.

Notre Dame College Prep Gala Video

Hello. My name is Pat McCaskey. I'm at home now. So this is a recording.

I work for the Chicago Bears and Notre Dame College Prep. On Friday, June 6, 1967, at 7:00 p.m., I graduated from Notre Dame High School.

Notre Dame College Prep has been very, very good to me. I received an excellent education and faith development.

Notre Dame College Prep has an excellent Chairman, Kevin Burke; an excellent President, Shay Boyle; and an excellent Principal, Dan Tully. They remind me of the Trinity and not the three stooges.

When I was a Notre Dame High School sophomore, my writing teacher, Father Sandonato, said to me, "McCaskey, you have a unique writing talent. You should develop it."

I replied, "Father, I have to get to practice." Now I am the author of nine books.

Jesus said eternal life is a banquet. May the 30th Spirit Gala be a preview of Heaven.

Thank you for listening. This is better than talking to myself. It's great to be with you. Have a Hall of Fame night.

One Good Deed Leads to Another

In 1926, my grandfather, George Halas, hired Honey Russell to coach the Chicago Bruins, a professional basketball team. In 1928, Honey Russell played in one game for the Chicago Bears.

From 1939-1942, Honey Russell coached Bob Davies in basketball at Seton Hall. Bob Davies became the model for Chip Hilton in the 24-book Sports Series that Clair Bee wrote. In *Fourth Down Showdown*, sports columnist Bill Bell wrote that Chip Hilton ran like Red Grange and passed like Sid Luckman.

During World War II, Bob Davies was in the Navy. He helped track enemy submarines. From 1946-1955, he played for the Rochester Royals, a professional basketball team.

My cousin, Phil McCaskey, caddied for Bob Cousy and Bob Davies at Lancaster Country Club. My brother, Mike McCaskey, said that my uncle, Tom McCaskey, was the Club champion.

Packers-Bears Sportsmanship Event

On Saturday, January 2, 2020, at 7:00 p.m., there was a zoom event to promote the sportsmanship in the Packers-Bears rivalry. What is now the National Football League started in 1920. The Bears were a charter franchise. The Packers joined the league in 1921. The Packers are doing very well for an expansion franchise.

Sports Faith International hosted the event. Sports Faith recognizes people who are successful in sports while leading exemplary lives. We honor high school, college, and professional athletes, coaches, and teams on Pentecost Vigil.

Sports Faith has a radio station, WSFI, 88.5 FM. The tower is in Antioch, Illinois, and the studio is in Libertyville, Illinois. We broadcast in northern Illinois and southern Wisconsin. All WSFI listeners are cordially invited to participate in the zoom event.

All donors to WSFI will receive a copy of my book *Sportsmanship.* It has a cover picture of George Halas and Vince Lombardi.

George Halas and Vince Lombardi had great respect for each other. Both of them are in the Sports Faith Hall of Fame.

TUITION REBATE

On January 22, 1972, my grandfather, George Halas, gave a speech in Washington, DC. Here is an excerpt.

"Once I had a great friend who passed for too short a time on this earth, in this country, in this city. Once he said: 'Football symbolizes the attributes of America: stamina, courage, teamwork, self-denial, sportsmanship, selflessness, and respect for authority.'

"My friend's name was Vince Lombardi."

John Lombardi was the visiting team for this event so he called the coin toss to determine who would speak first. Each of us spoke for fifteen minutes because that is how long it took for the Sermon on Mount. I wasn't there but I typed it and timed it because I wanted to know how long it took for the best sermon. Listeners had opportunities to ask questions for thirty minutes.

A Poetic Potpourri from Pond Three

In nineteen fourteen, Cleveland engineer
Jim Hoge invented the stoplight with a
Red light and a green light. Detroit police-
man William Potts added a yellow light.

Seamus Heaney explained the difference
Between optimism and hope. Optimism
Says that everything will be grand and hope
Explains why something is worth working for.

The worst part of Dante's Hell is quite cold.
My goal is to become mature, not old.
Hear God gladly; we won't be crotchety.
Jackie Gleason said, "And away we go."

The Everly Brothers sang "Why Worry."
McFerrin sang "Don't Worry, Be Happy."

Community High School All-Stars

The Chicago Bears have programs that support and praise young athletes. On February 4, 2021, the Bears honored community high school all-stars. With no Friday night games that fall, the 2020 All-Stars were selected due to helping their communities. Here is my congratulatory speech.

My grandfather, George Halas, started the Bears in 1920. He played on the team for 10 years. He coached the team for 40 years. He was the owner of the team for 62 years until he died in 1983 at the age of 88. He often said, "Life is too short for grudges."

To his family, he also said, "May the good Lord grant all of you as long and as wonderful a life as I have had."

He left the team to his family. We are trying to extend his legacy. That legacy has two parts: win championships and help other people.

Congratulations to all of you Community High School All-Stars. Your accomplishments are exemplary.

George Halas went to Crane Tech High School in Chicago. All of you are like a young George Halas.

Hall of Fame Bears' linebacker, Mike Singletary was also on hand to speak on-line with the athletes. Here is my introduction of Mike Singletary.

In 1981, Mike Singletary was a second-round draft choice of the Bears. He played middle linebacker for the Bears from 1981 through 1992. He played on the Bears' 1985 championship team. He played in ten Pro Bowls. He was All Pro nine times. He was the Walter Payton Man of the Year once. He was the NFL Defensive Player of the Year twice. He was the NFC Player of the Year three times. He was the NFL

Linebacker of the Year twice. He made the NFL 1980s All-Decade Team. He is number 15 on the top 100 Bears of All-Time. He won the Bart Starr Award once. He is a Pro Football Hall of Famer.

When Mike played for the Bears, he and I lived in the same subdivision. We have the same Saviour. If Mike had been one of the original Apostles, the other Apostles wouldn't have slept in the Garden of Gethsemane.

Here's a quote from Mike on the occasion:

"To be able to make a difference and make an impact when there's so many other things going on this year in this pandemic, is absolutely exemplary. It's absolutely amazing that young people can have the vision, discipline and awareness to be able to think about others in a time when everybody is just kind of scrambling to stay afloat."

Here are the community high school all-stars who were honored: Eric Moreno, Fenton; A J Wrenn, Saint Laurence; Nickolas Benn, Fenton; Carter Collins, Maine South; Jalen Aguilar, Whitney Young; Omarian James, Foreman; Blake Eversmann, Harrisburg; Miles McVay, East Saint Louis; James Gildersleeve, Lake Forest.

Douglass Park Field Dedication

When my grandfather, George Halas, was a student-athlete at Crane Tech, he lived in an apartment at 18th Place and Wood in Chicago.[29] When he started the Bears in Chicago, he lived at 4356 Washington Boulevard.

---

[29] Crane Tech is now known as Crane Medical Preparatory High School.

Ninety-two Chicago Bears have played high school football in the state of Illinois. That includes seven Pro Football Hall of Famers: Dick Butkus, George Connor, Paddy Driscoll, Red Grange, George Halas, George Musso, and George Trafton. Before they reached high school and ultimately the NFL, they got their starts in the parks and backyards of their hometown neighborhoods. I would venture to say though, that their parks and backyards never looked like this!

The Bears are pleased to celebrate the dedication of this Douglass Park field. The Chicago Bears and Bears Care have a long history of supporting youth football programming and are excited to be able to expand our investment in the game and Chicago's children with this field. We know that athletics pay dividends in the lives of young people, their healthy development and the unity and vibrancy of their communities. We hope the field will serve not only as a great home for spirited athletic competition, but for community events and family activities in the years ahead.

Healthy communities need good housing, good schools, good jobs, and good places to play. Bears Care and the Chicago Bears are committed to investing in Chicago neighborhoods and Chicago youth. Let this field be a reminder: God performs miracles for people of faith who diligently work together. Let sportsmanship prevail.

Confirmation Anniversary 4.20.21

Now is the anniversary of our Confirmation.

The soldiers who were stationed at the Tomb were given bribes to say that the body of Jesus was stolen. Soldiers of Christ do not take bribes, but we're allowed to accept Confirmation gifts.

My Confirmation name is Paul.

Annette Funicello had a song called "Tall Paul."

Don Rickles and George Scott were classmates at the American Academy of Dramatic Arts. When George Scott was in the Eugene O'Neill play "Desire Under the Elms," he received a call from Don Rickles.

Don Rickles invited George Scott to leave the play to be in a movie. Don said, "It's a small part and there isn't much money, but it's a chance to work with Annette Funicello."

Renewed by His Strength

Isaiah 40:31, "They that hope in the Lord will renew their strength, they will soar as with eagles' wings; they will run and not grow weary, walk and not grow faint."

For six days a week,
I exercise vigorously.
Even God took a day off.
I was made
In His image.
When I listen
To my body,
I hear the ocean.
When I hold a conch (sea shell)
To my ear,
I hear Eric Liddell run.
On the day
Of rest,
I am God's guest.
I am renewed by His Strength.

Something Wonderful

On an early Monday afternoon, I went to Saint Pat's Church to retrieve my "Magnificat." I had left it in the pew after morning Mass.

Jose Felix was vacuuming the Church. He stopped because he thought that I needed quiet in order to pray.

I explained that I was just there to get my "Magnificat." He cheerfully resumed vacuuming.

Shall We Eat a Piece of Liver

Shall we eat a piece of liver
We have planted some new sod
No more arrows in our quiver
The new grass will be grown by God

Yes, we'll eat a piece of liver
The ketchup-soaked, the ketchup-soaked liver
We will be saints when we eat liver
We offer it up to God

Soon we'll eat the tasty liver
Soon our sacrifice will cease
Soon the waitress will deliver
Some dessert to give us peace

Yes, we'll eat a piece of liver
The ketchup-soaked, the ketchup-soaked liver
We will be saints when we eat liver
We offer it up to God

HARD KNOCKS

When Christ was in Galilee synagogues,
All of His listeners glorified Him.
Then He went to teach His Hometown.
The people there were a tough crowd.

First, He read from the Book of Isaiah.
Then He sat down and talked to His people.
They remembered Him as son of Joseph.
They did not see Him as the Messiah.

People of Nazareth were narrow-minded.
They did not accept Jesus Christ.

—PKPMc

Many books have been written about why bad things happen to good people. It is something many of us struggle through. When we live through hard times there are lessons to learn. In sports, some like to say that a loss provides lessons that a win can never provide.

Some people help us prepare for the battles we will face. They help us become tougher and more resilient.

Tom Thayer's Excellent Remembrance of Clyde Emrich

On Tuesday, November 16, 2021, the funeral Mass for Clyde Emrich took place at Saint Joseph Catholic Church in Libertyville. After Communion, Tom Thayer delivered his excellent remembrance of Clyde.

Patrick McCaskey

You are lucky in life if you are able to surround yourself with positive people who happen to be parents, brothers, sisters, and friends. Even luckier if those people become your mentors. Even more fortunate if those mentors help guide the course of your life.

Little did I know as a 14-year old boy from Joliet that I would meet a legend...THE LEGEND!!!

Francis Ruettiger drove me to the Bears' training camp at Lake Forest College. We stopped at a gas station and asked for directions. Clyde was wearing a Bears' shirt and so we asked him. He had us follow him in his car to the camp and he showed us where to park.

My chance meeting with Clyde would bear fruit a decade later when I joined the Bears.

I was a weight room guy. I lived there and bonded with Clyde, creating a lifelong friendship, I will forever cherish.

It is where I learned that winning, and success starts in the weight room. It's not just a physical pursuit, it is a mental pursuit.

I can still hear him. I will always hear him. We will always hear him.

"The strong defeat the weak and the smart defeat the strong," Clyde would say.

It crystalized the idea that strength is both mind and body. You get yelled at by Coach Ditka or a Hall of Famer like offensive line coach Dick Stanfel, learn from it, and don't crumble under the criticism.

"Knowledge earned is greater than knowledge learned."

Take it from the meeting room to the practice field, but learn what it takes to survive in battle when fatigue can make cowards of us all. What happens on Sunday is a unique opportunity on every single snap.

"You can't shoot a cannon from a canoe."

TUITION REBATE

Your physique may look good coming off the bus, but it's your base, your lower half strength that gives you the power to win your battles. Leg strength is #1.

"You can't pull a semi with a Volkswagen engine."

Clyde learned from an early age that what drives you makes you stronger and makes you better. The hardest thing to measure in an athlete is the size of his heart. The work ethic must be consistent and purposeful and meet the demands of the sport.

All of that knowledge was poured into all of us here. It may have been phrased in different ways to different people, but the message was the same.

Clyde set the example every day. He treated everyone equally from the stars to the last man on the roster, to every person in the building or outside the building. You see, Clyde was not just developing stronger players, he was developing people. If you listened, you came away a better person.

Clyde's loyalty to the Bears covered 7 decades and will continue in perpetuity! His words were teachings, but his actions spoke louder. That is also revealed in his love for sons Kenny and John and their families.

For a quarter of a century every Monday and Tuesday, I drove to Halas to get there by 6 am; not because I had to, but because I wanted to. We sat in the video department. We talked about the Bears. We talked about life. And we all walked away better because of it.

Clyde Emrich's bio begins this way: "The first man in the world." It tells you how accomplished and special he was in the history of weightlifting. Clyde Emrich was the Best Man in the World to me. He was my friend.

The National Football League, the Chicago Bears, and everyone here are better for having known him, to be impacted by him, and to have walked with him through life's peaks and valleys. Heaven awaits and he will no doubt be heard to say, "good lift, good lift."

Clyde has been lifting all of us to be better, be stronger, and to reach higher. He was a true blessing, a gift for all to enjoy.

Steve "Mongo" McMichael

Steve McMichael was born in Houston, Texas. His family moved 100 miles due south from San Antonio to Freer, Texas. McMichael played six sports at Freer High School including football. He was highly recruited by colleges. He attended the University of Texas and played defensive tackle for the Longhorns. In college, he was a consensus All American who would later be inducted into the College Hall of Fame.

McMichael was drafted and played for the New England Patriots in 1980 and he played one year for the Green Bay Packers in 1994. He was all-Bears in the seasons between: 1981-1993. McMichael said the Bears were a good team for him because they judged you by how you played.

It was 1983 when "No. 76" broke into the starting lineup. In his 13 years on the Bears, McMichael had 92.5 sacks, 814 tackles, 3 safeties, and 2 interceptions. He was an All Pro twice and invited to the Pro Bowl twice. McMichael played a key role for the Bears in their 1985 Championship season. McMichael played alongside Dan Hampton, Richard Dent, and William Perry on the defensive line.

McMichael was named one of the Top 100 Bears Players in Franchise History selected by Dan Pompei and Don Pierson.

Mike Ditka called McMichael the toughest player he ever coached. Early in 2021, McMichael was diagnosed with ALS, also known as Lou Gehrig's disease. The Bears, teammates, and fans reached out in support of McMichael and his family.

Bronislau "Bronko" Nagurski

The early days of pro football were difficult. George Halas and others were doing everything they could to keep the National Football League afloat. It would be decades before financial success came. Early players were paid by the game and the offseason was time for another job. Even the stars of the game faced financial difficulties with some exceptions.

Halas himself knew players from the early days to modern times. He said the early players were in a class by themselves, certainly the toughest to play the game. And among those, no one was tougher than Bronko Nagurski.

Nagurski was one of the biggest stars of the 1930s. He was born in Rainy River, Ontario, Canada. His parents emigrated from Eastern Europe, the Ukraine. The family moved to International Falls, Minnesota, a place of frigid winters nicknamed the Icebox of the Nation. The family had a farm and Nagurski got bigger and stronger working the land.

Nagurski went to high school at Bemidji High School in his final year to attract college scouts. He attended the University of Minnesota where he was an All American at both fullback and tackle. Nagurski was signed-up by George Halas after college.

Bronko played for the Bears from 1931-1937 and was back again in 1943. He was a one-of-a-kind fullback and a tackle/linebacker. "Bronk" had the size, strength, and speed of modern fullbacks coupled with the toughness of a freight train. Like many players of the Era, he played both sides of the ball. He was what the sports writers would call a complete player.

Opposing teams prepared for a Nagurski charge up the middle so a particularly effective play had Nagurski fake the run, pedal backwards, jump for a clear view of the receiver, and throw a pass. Mostly, Nagurski would run people over. He would carry the ball or clear a lane for other runners like Beattie Feathers, the first running back to top 1,000 yards in a season. On defense, he would plug the holes up.

After retirement from football, beloved Bronko was coaxed back to the Bears in 1943 to help them win the Championship that year. Nagurski was an All Pro four times. Rushing stats from the 1930s don't translate well in modern days, but Nagurski had four seasons where he rushed for over 500 yards and in many rushing categories for several seasons he ranked in the top ten. He had 25 rushing touchdowns. Bronko played on three Bears Championships: 1932, 1933, and 1943. He is on the Hall of Fame 1930s Team. Nagurski was inducted into the Pro Football Hall of Fame in the Charter Class of 1963. Nagurski is one of the Top 100 Players in Bears History.

Nagurski was always looking to earn more money for his family. He became a professional wrestler. He was a professional athlete for three decades. He continued farming and owned a gas station.

If you ever get up by International Falls, Minnesota, you might like to visit the Bronko Nagurski Museum at 214 6th Avenue. The museum is attached to the Koochiching Historical Museum. Nagurski never moved from the area. His family donated much of his memorabilia to the museum after his death.

TUITION REBATE

Matt Forte

> *Matt Forte loved playing football*
> *With a love as big as the sky*
> *Matt Forte loved playing football*
> *With a love that didn't die*
>
> —PKPMc

Matt Forte's life is far different than Bronko Nagurski's, but sacrifice is also at the heart of it. For Forte, it is about the sacrifices his parents made for him that helped him to become an athlete who played for a decade at the highest level of professional football.

Forte grew up in Slidell, Louisiana. He went to Slidell High School where he lettered in football, and track and field. For college, he went to Tulane where he rushed for 2,000 yards as a senior.

Forte was a second round draft choice of the Bears in 2008. Forte's performance would work out exactly where he would be placed in the pantheon of Bear running backs. In eight seasons for the Bears, Forte rushed 2,035 times for 8,602 yards and 45 touchdowns. As a receiver, he was targeted 636 times and had 487 receptions for 4,116 yards and 19 touchdowns. Forte was a fast, powerful runner who was durable. He was a complete modern back because he was an excellent receiver as well.

Upon his retirement from football in 2018, Bears Chairman George McCaskey praised Forte's legacy with the Bears, lauding the former running back as "a superior athlete and frequently the best player on the field."

97

Where Does Forte Rank?

Forte ranks second on the Bears' all-time list behind Hall of Famer Walter Payton in rushing yards and several other categories by which a running back is measured today.

Lively Virtues Overcome Deadly Sins

Chastity, no escaping that for me.
Lust is a bust that betrays heaven's trust.
Temperance or self-restraint is not quaint.
Gluttony involves too much quantity.

Charity means love of God and neighbor.
Greed is the wanting of more than we need.
Diligence is a careful persistence.
Sloth refuses the joy that comes from God.

Patience is forbearance, not annoyance.
Wrath at her hurts me like a catheter.
Kindness helps the deaf hear and the blind see.
Envy can motivate us to improve.

Humility is thanks for deity.
Pride is unjustified self-confidence.

Sports Faith Banquet

As the Chair of Sports Faith International, I host various events like their annual banquet.

2021 Sports Faith Awards Ceremony

The Sports Faith Awards Ceremony was on Pentecost Vigil, Saturday, May 22, 2021, at the Doubletree Inn

TUITION REBATE

Pleasant Prairie, Wisconsin. Father Dwight Campbell who is a spiritual advisor to WSFI 88.5 FM, from the Archdiocese of Milwaukee, said the opening prayer.

Dan Miller is the state director for Pro-Life Wisconsin. He led us in the Pledge of Allegiance. Sela Goodloe, who is a senior at Carmel High School in Mundelein sang the National Anthem.

Catholic Memorial High School
Catholic Memorial High School is located in Waukesha, Wisconsin. The School's Varsity Girls Soccer Team received the All Star Catholic Lifetime Achievement Award. Varsity Girls Soccer compete athletically, grow academically, and live through service. They win championships. They are brilliant in the classroom. They serve the community. They do all three at the highest possible level. Catholic Memorial High School has sixteen Wisconsin state championships, six of which were consecutive. They have been an Academic All-American team 21 times. They have the all-time winning percentage (.794) among schools with at least 300 wins. They donate their time to TOP Soccer, a program that teaches the sport to children with special needs.

Andrean High School
Andrean High School is located in Merrillville, Indiana. Dave Pishkur is in his 41st orbit as the Varsity Head Baseball Coach of the Andrean 59ers. He played on the 59ers first baseball team. He is a 1971 Andrean graduate. He played baseball and golf for Purdue University Calumet. In 1998, in honor of his mother and the mother of God, Dave obtained the donations and free labor to build a grotto at Andrean. He and his wife, Gretchen, have three children. Pishkur was presented with the All

Star Catholic High School Coaching Lifetime Achievement Award. He is the Indiana all-time wins leader with 1,014. He is in the Max Preps top 100 coaches in high school sports. Andrean High School has won seven Indiana state championships.

Saint Michael the Archangel

Sports Faith International All Star Catholic High School Award was presented to Saint Michael the Archangel located in Fredericksburg, Virginia. Hugh Brown is a founder, chairman, and football coach at the school. In 2019, they won the Virginia state championship with 17 players, all of whom were well coached. Hugh says, "Football is the vehicle. Christ is the destination." Hugh played football at the University of Maryland. He and his wife, Ann, have five children. He and his mother, American Life League founder, Judie Brown, are known for their entrepreneurial spirit, courage, and straight-talk, especially in the advancement of the culture of life.

Deacon Steve Javie

Deacon Steve Javie was presented with the Father Smyth Award. Father Smyth was an All-American basketball player for the University of Notre Dame. He was a first-round NBA draft choice who gave up professional basketball after a year to become a priest. He helped build Maryville Academy. He helped save Notre Dame College Prep. He helped the Standing Tall Foundation to stand tall. Deacon Javie played football, basketball, and baseball for LaSalle High School in Philadelphia. He played baseball for Temple University and played in the minor leagues for the Baltimore Orioles. He was a 25-year NBA referee. In 2019, Archbishop Charles J. Chaput ordained Steve as a deacon for Saint Andrew Parish in Newton, Pennsylvania. Steve and his wife, Mary Ellen, live in Langhorne, Pennsylvania.

TUITION REBATE

Rich Gannon

Rich Gannon was inducted into the Sports Faith International Hall of Fame for Professional Football. When he was a child, he wrote a report on the saintly life of Bishop Saint John Neumann. Copies are available upon request. He was a three-sport athlete (football, basketball, and crew) for Saint Joseph Preparatory School in Philadelphia. He played football for the University of Delaware. In 1987, he was a fourth-round draft choice of the New England Patriots. Gannon played quarterback for the Minnesota Vikings, Washington Redskins, Kansas City Chiefs, and Oakland Raiders. He played 18 seasons. He played in four Pro Bowls. Gannon was All Pro twice, NFL MVP once, and an NFL champion once. He was a 16-year CBS Sports commentator. Gannon and his wife, Shelley, have two daughters. He says the rosary every day. He listens to broadcasts of Bishop Sheen. Gannon expresses his faith very well. He is a wonderful example of perseverance and sportsmanship.

Jim Grabowski

Jim Grabowski was inducted into the Sports Faith International Hall of Fame for Professional Football. Grabowski was a three-sport athlete (football, basketball, and track) for Taft High School in Chicago. He played football for the University of Illinois, the Green Bay Packers, and the Chicago Bears. Grabowski was an All American, an Academic All American, a Rose Bowl Most Valuable Player, and a Big Ten Most Valuable Player. He was a first-round draft choice of the Packers. He played on two Packer NFL Championship teams. The Packers are doing very well for an expansion team. Grabowski is in the Academic American Hall of Fame, the Polish American Sports Hall of Fame, the Chicago

Sports Hall of Fame, and the National Football Foundation College Hall of Fame. Now he is a Sports Faith Hall of Famer. Grabowski provided color commentary for the University of Illinois football radio broadcasts from 1974 through 2006. He has been married for 54 years to his high school sweetheart, Kathy. They had a very nice time at their prom. They have two daughters.

Bishop Thomas John Paprocki

Bishop Thomas John Paprocki is a native Chicagoan. Now he is doing missionary work among the politicians in Springfield. He is the Episcopal Advisor to Sports Faith International. He is a Sports Faith Hall of Famer. The world is a better place because he is the author of two books: *Holy Goals for Body and Soul* and *Running for a Higher Purpose*. These books will help us get to Heaven. Bishop Paprocki blessed us and said the closing prayer.

The Ten Plagues of Egypt

The ten plagues of Egypt were
Blood,
Frogs,
Gnats,
Flies,
Livestock,
Boils,
Hail,
Locusts,
Darkness, and
First-born deaths.

In a hit song the Gershwins queried,
"Who could ask for anything more?"

Thoughts at Recess

Workouts are recess. I thank God and my doctors for my health.

John Wooden said that you can't give more than 100%. I give 100%.

Sometimes when I run, I feel like I'm flying on the wings of Pegasus. Other times I feel like Babe Ruth chugging around the bases after he had hit a home run.

Ties for First

In 1936, in the USA Olympic Trials 5,000-meter run, Don Lash and Louie Zamperini tied for first.

In 1965, in the AAU Championship six-mile run, Gerry Lindgren and Billy Mills tied for first.

In 1967, in the Choate triangular cross-country meet, Alan Swanson and I tied for first.

In 1972, in the USA Olympic Trials marathon, Kenny Moore and Frank Shorter tied for first.

Two Exceptional High School Principals

My great, great grandfather, J. P. McCaskey, was a teacher and a principal for over 50 years at Boys High School in Lancaster, Pennsylvania. To each graduate of the high school, he gave a coin. One side had this inscription: "The best of men that ever wore earth about him was a patient sufferer, a soft, meek, tranquil Spirit, the first true gentleman that ever breathed."

That was written about Jesus. My great, great grandfather never even met me. On the other side of the coin was a portrait of J. P. with this quote, "I am one of Jack's boys."

Father Smyth hired Dan Tully to be a teacher and a principal at Notre Dame College Prep. What an excellent decision. Graduates can gratefully say, "We are Danny's boys."

Principal Dan Tully

Oh Danny's boys, Dear God, Dear God is calling
From town to town, and in the cities too.
The football's gone, and all the records falling
'Tis you, 'tis you must go and share the faith.

FAMILY LESSONS

Noah and family entered the ark.
There were two dogs, male and female, to bark.
Noah and family survived the flood.
For a long time, there was a lot of mud.

—PKPMc

Most of us learn from our home and family. We can learn by what our parents and siblings say, but we learn by example as well. Good examples help.

"The Rosary Priest," Father Patrick Peyton, pioneered Catholic media in the 1940s on the radio and then television. One radio show featured Archbishop Francis Spellman of New York and President Harry Truman who spoke about the importance of family prayer.[30] Father Peyton's motto was "The family that prays together stays together."

What I Learned from My Grandparents

My father's father, Grandpa Dick (McCaskey), taught me how to play Solitaire. My mother's father, Grandpa George (Halas), taught me how to persevere. Now I play Solitaire until I win.

My mother's mother, Grandma Min (Halas), taught me how to enjoy my family. At a family gathering, my sister Mary and her dog Fagan did a series of tricks: heal, sit, lie down, roll over, and shake.

---

[30] Spellman would become a Cardinal in 1946.

Then my brother Ned and my brother George said, "What's so hard about that?"

Ned was the dog trainer and George was the dog. They did the same tricks and Grandma Min laughed with great appreciation.

My father's mother, Grandma Kit (McCaskey), told me what she wanted on her tombstone: "I tried."

Grandpa George lived to be 88 years old. He often said, "Life is too short for grudges."

What I'm Learning During the Quarantine

"The Divine Comedy" is not funny.
It's about Hell, Purgatory, and Heaven.

Mark Twain said, "There's no humor in Heaven."
He also said, "When we get to Heaven,
We will study and study and study
And progress and progress and progress and
If that isn't Hell, I don't know what is."

The Bible does not have a lot of laughs.
There are birds on the pond but no giraffes.
There are cranes. George Halas went to Crane Tech.
After our chores are done, card games are fun.
Marriage is better than living alone.
Emails are helpful and so is the phone.
Skypes help us see how grandchildren have grown.

Mugs Halas

On September 4, 1925, George Halas Junior, "Mugs," was born in Chicago. He went to Loyola Academy when it was in Chicago. He was my brother Mike's godfather. During World War II, his father, George Halas, who was a Naval Officer at the time, inducted him into the

Navy. From April 5, 1944, through October 14, 1945, Grandpa wrote 28 letters to Mugs from on board ship in the South Pacific.

President Truman sent this letter to George Stanley Halas, Junior:

"To you who answered the call of your country and served in its Armed Forces to bring about the total defeat of the enemy, I extend the heartfelt thanks of a grateful Nation. As one of the Nation's finest, you undertook the most severe task one can be called upon to perform. Because you demonstrated the fortitude, resourcefulness and calm judgment necessary to carry out that task, we now look to you for leadership and example in further exalting our country in peace."

After we won the war, Mugs finished his undergraduate studies at Loyola University Chicago. He started working for the Bears in 1950. Max Swiatek gave him a broom to sweep out the back room.[31]

Mugs became the Bears' treasurer in 1953. When the Bears won the 1963 NFL Championship, he was the team's President and General Manager. He was on the Executive Committee of the NFL Management Council.

In 1967, Mugs hired my father, Ed McCaskey, to be the Bears' Vice President and Treasurer. In 1974, Mugs hired Jim Finks to be the Bears' Executive Vice President, General Manager, and Chief Operating Officer.

On December 16, 1979, Mugs died of a heart attack at the age of 54. He is remembered for his devotion to the Bears and to the NFL.

---

[31] Swiatek is the number one employee on the Bears longevity list with 67 years' service. Swiatek was hired by Halas and served as a great example of someone who was willing to tackle many jobs for the good of the team.

When Bob Kilcullen played for the Bears, he took art classes at the Art Institute in Chicago. After Mugs had died, Bob made a portrait of Mugs and gave it to his father.[32]

On September 2, 1982, the George Halas Junior Sports Center was dedicated at Loyola University Chicago.

Walter Halas

On January 15, 1892, Walter Halas, my grandfather's older brother, was born at his home at 18th Place and Wood in Chicago. From 1914 through 1916, he was a varsity pitcher at the University of Illinois.

After Walter had graduated in 1916, he pitched for the Davenport Blue Sox, the Moline Plowboys, and the Rock Island Islanders of the Illinois-Indiana-Iowa League. Then he went to Somerset, Kentucky, where he coached the Somerset High School football and baseball teams. From there, he coached at Davenport High School. He met his wife, Ann McGuirk, who was a teacher there. He persuaded Elmer Layden, a later member of the famed Four-Horsemen, to go to Notre Dame.

From 1919 through 1922, Walter was Knute Rockne's assistant at Notre Dame. Walter was also the basketball and baseball coach there. My grandfather asked Walter to attend games involving teams the Bears would soon meet. Walter's reports won many games for the Bears.

After Notre Dame, Walter was the athletic director and football coach at Mount Saint Mary's in Maryland. From 1924 through 1927, he was the athletic director,

---

[32] Kilcullen was a defensive lineman who played for the Bears from 1957 through 1968, with the exception of 1959.

basketball coach, and baseball coach at Haverford. From 1927 through 1941, he coached football, basketball, and baseball at Drexel Institute in Philadelphia.

On February 13, 1923, my mother was baptized at Saint Mel's Church in Chicago. Walter was her godfather. My grandfather insisted that my mother attend Drexel because he knew that Walter would look after her.

In 1942, Walter was the freshman coach under Clark Shaughnessy at the University of Maryland. Grandpa wrote to Walter from the Pacific and told him the Bears needed help and asked him to lend a hand. Walter resigned from Maryland and came to the Bears as a Vice-President. He also looked after the sporting goods business and became a trusted and valuable scout for the team. He worked on obtaining school and college athletic uniform business. At the same time, he was the Bears' chief scout on game days.

On December 4, 1959, he had a heart attack. He died on December 20, 1959, in Chicago at the age of 67. He was buried at Mount Calvary Catholic Cemetery in Davenport.

Frank Halas

On September 7, 1882, Frank Halas, my grandfather's oldest brother, was born in Chicago. He was named after his father. Frank attended Joseph Medill High School at West 14th and South Loomis. He played football, basketball, and baseball. After he had graduated, he played semipro football and baseball.

After my grandfather had graduated from Crane Tech, Frank suggested that Grandpa should work for a year before he went to the University of Illinois. That would be an opportunity for Grandpa to gain weight to play football. That's what happened.

From 1896 through 1928, Frank played semi-pro softball. He may have been the best softball pitcher of all time. In one game, he had 29 strikeouts.

Frank had elected not to go to college. He opted for a job at the Post Office with its longevity and future pension. Frank worked for the Chicago Post Office until he retired in 1944.

Frank handled the Bears' travel arrangements from 1922 through 1971. He distributed per diem to the players who called him Uncle Frank. He said to the bus drivers, "Buse, you can start the bus when I tell you, you can start the bus. Okay, start the bus."

He made certain to collect the Bears' share of the gate before the Bears left town. Then the payroll could be met the following Monday. During his tenure, the Bears went from railroad day-coach travel to chartered jet planes.

Frank oversaw the home-game preparations. He hired many people on a one-day basis for the Bears' home games. He manned the Bears' pass gate at Wrigley Field. He was very gracious when my family brought friends to the games.

Frank and his first wife, Mamie O'Conner, had a daughter, Mary Barbara Halas. After Mamie had died, he married Alice Richardson.

On January 10, 1972, Frank died in Chicago at the age of 89. The wake was at W. C. Smith and Sons Funeral Home, 2500 North Cicero Avenue. The funeral was at Saint Canisius Church, 5057 West North Avenue. He and both of his wives have been interred in the Halas Mausoleum at Saint Adalbert Catholic Cemetery in Niles, Illinois.

Wedding Anniversary 3.3.21

On March 3, 1984, Gretchen and I married each other. Our mutual friend, Reverend Wayne Gordon, was the minister. My grade school friend, Father Don Nevins, was the priest.

Gretchen wore a gown fashioned of white chiffon and styled with a wedding-band neckline, short puffed sleeves, a chapel train, and an embroidered jacket with peplum.

Her long illusion veil fell from a Juliet cap fashioned of embroidered chiffon with chiffon ruching.

She carried a bouquet of white roses, stephanotis, and babies' breath.

I remember how beautiful she was and is.

At the reception, my late brother Mike gave a speech about me with a lot of flattery. Many people asked, "Who's he talking about?"

Jim & Emily

When Clare and Nancy Croghan were matriculating at Woodlands Academy in Lake Forest, they worked for the Chicago Bears at Lake Forest College after school. I asked them if I could please speak at their school. They said sure, but it never happened.

After Nancy Croghan Sheridan's daughter, Emily, began teaching at Saint Mary of the Angels School in Chicago, I asked Emily if I could please speak at her school. She said sure, but the school told Emily that I had already spoken there, twice.

I wanted to get married when I was in eighth grade because my parents had a great marriage. For my 33rd birthday, my uncle, Jim McCaskey, gave me permission to date.

After nine months of prayer, I met Gretchen Wagle through mutual friends, the Bradleys and the Swiders. Four months later, we looked at the Siffermann's house because it was for sale.

After the tour, Gretchen asked me, "Why are you looking for a house?"

I crossed my mouth with the back of my right hand and muttered, "In case you want to get married." She accepted my invitation.

When my son's age was in single digits, I asked him if I could please call him Jim. He asked, "Can I have a dog?"

James applied to seven colleges. My plan for him was to have a semester at each college. For the eighth semester, I would homeschool him and he would be valedictorian.

After he had earned a master's degree and after he had become a certified public accountant, he ran away from home.

My plan for him was to get married and have children and we would all live together in the same house like the Waltons. Children don't always do what their parents want them to do.

And yet, children are a blessing. They grow up and they get married. If they are blessed with children, we hope and trust that the parents will provide accountability and encouragement for the children.

In preparation for marrying Emily, Jim developed physically, socially, culturally, and spiritually. I am grateful to Jim for being my son. I am grateful to Emily for accepting Jim's invitation.

Tom McCaskey's Best Man Speech

Growing up with Eddie and James, I cannot imagine too many people had a better childhood than the three of us. Throw in a summer cameo from our cousins Daniel and Brandon, and we were just in heaven. The majority of our childhood was spent in our basement away from our arch nemesis the sun. For the most part we were making up games and watching the Olsen twins solve crimes before dinner time. My favorite memory from the basement, we had a Fisher Price mini-pool table, and James must have lost 97 games in a row. He just couldn't get a win, and it probably didn't help that he was playing pool lefty. I remember the day James was finally triumphant over Eddie. The loss caused Eddie to turn the pool cue into a javelin and throw it through our basement wall.

On the days it was a little overcast and we were brave enough to fight the sun, we would be outside having home run derbies and practicing our knuckle pucks. The one thing I love the most was playing basketball with my little brother. We played every game to 11, and when one of us actually won we had a million rules to just keep the game going. It would be fadeaway threes or some long toss; just anything to keep the game going in order that I could spend more time playing with my brother.

My brothers and I would fish in our backyard. The key to catching bluegills in our pond was to use the fat free Kraft cheese. Not because the fish like it more, but because we knew if we didn't use it for fishing then we would have to use the fat free brand for our grilled cheeses. As we grew older, Eddie and James stuck with fishing, and I would hang out inside whenever they would go out together. I remember one time when James

113

was fishing alone, I was playing Dave Mirra's Pro Skater. It didn't go great for them. So, I was playing fake Tony Hawk listening to Fall Out Boy because I am not a robot, and my little brother James comes running downstairs screaming in a way I have never seen before. He was shaking and yelling you have to come outside quickly. I was terrified; I thought something horrible had happened. While he was fishing, he had hooked a frog and couldn't get it off the line. I ran outside with him; we got the frog off the hook and placed it back in the pond.

You are probably thinking "He just told a story where he was the hero. That's probably not the right move. He's so vain he probably thought this speech was about him." I tell this story because this is honestly the only time I felt like an older brother to James. He has always been there for me when I needed him. Thank you, I love you James. Emily, I would say welcome to the family, but you have been a part of our family for so long and we are all so glad that it is finally official. Thank you for making him happier than anyone possibly could. Emily and James, I love you both so much.

Jim McCaskey's Groom Speech

Thank you all for being here, we are so happy to have all of our best friends and family to celebrate with us. None of this would be possible without Phil and Nancy; thank you for putting this together. This has been such an incredible night and so much hard work and preparation went into this. I couldn't ask for better in-laws. Nancy is probably the coolest mom I have ever met; she is always dancing and singing, and her kids worship her because she is an incredible person. Phil, I overcame one of my biggest fears in my life yesterday when you hosted the golf outing for all the groomsmen. I have turned him down maybe ten plus times for golf, and so this was a big moment for us. I have heard many times this weekend how Emily and I remind people of Phil and Nancy, which is such an honor to hear because you two are the best.

To my parents, Gretchen and Patrick, thank you so much for last night. Tom touched on our childhood during his speech, and I cannot thank you enough. You two are such examples of what it means to be great people and great parents especially. I am so thankful for you, and I love you both. To our grandparents: first to our grandparents who are no longer with us: Ed, Gilmour, Helen, Doc, BJ. Thank you for helping us become the people we are today. John and Rosie you are two of the most generous people I have ever met in my life. You have such an incredible family that I am so honored to be a part of now. My grandma Virginia is here! She is the ultimate role model that we all look up to. What a great example of what it means to raise a loving family. Thank you all so much.

To my brothers, Eddie and Tom, thank you both so much. Tom touched on our childhood, which was hectic to say the least. A house of three boys around the same age: there were a lot of fights, a lot of tears, and a lot of discipline from Pops. You two are incredible. Being the youngest, I always just wanted to do everything that you guys were doing. I wanted to play whatever sports you were playing; I wanted to study whatever you were studying. I always loved growing up that no matter what you were doing with friends, you never cared that I was around. I was this chubby little brother, and you had no problem with me tagging along. I love you both.

I want to thank Kevin Borah as well. We met early freshman year at Loyola and were instant friends. He's the best; I truly wouldn't be here without him. Kevin always gave me a hard time in high school and college because I went behind his back with his cousin Emily. I never asked his permission to date her, so here I am publicly apologizing to you, Kevin. Thankfully, I ultimately received his blessing to marry Emily.

To my new siblings who have been like family for years; I love you all more than you'll ever know. I remember when Emily and I first started dating in high school. I would go over to the Sheridans' house, and we would all hang around their large kitchen table. There was shrieking, screaming, and they communicated in their own language basically. It was tough to follow what was happening at any given moment. I would hang out there for a few hours, maybe say two sentences, then kiss Emily and go home. On those long drives back to Lake Forest I would think to myself, "This is what it's like to have a girlfriend." Just as how my relationship with Emily has grown over time, it has with all of you. I confidently say now I have a unique, individual relationship with all of you, and I love you all so much.

Finally, to my wife. It is almost 10 years ago since I picked Emily up from Michigan Shores, drove her home, and asked her to be my girlfriend for the first time. I didn't know it at the time, but I had already found my wife. It's incredible to think about that. Kevin is laughing that I said the "first" time I asked her to be my girlfriend. As many of you know, I ended up asking her this multiple times throughout our relationship together. What I loved and cherished about our relationship was the fact we found each other so early on in our lives. We were able to grow individually during those formidable high school and college years, and even during times when we weren't together I felt so close to you.

It's funny though, it seems like no matter what happened we were destined to be together. Abbey mentioned in her speech the eighth-grade football game where the legend of the Black Northface was born. After that year, I moved on to Loyola and became friends with her cousin Kevin through Tom's best friend Brian Borah. After graduating from Loyola, Emily, Kevin, and I all ended up at Boston College where Emily's mom went to school. That being said, I think the biggest sign of destiny to me was the nickname my mom had for me growing up, which was Jama Lamba. I hated this nickname, but in recent years I found out the Sheridans had a pet llama growing up. It was named Jama the Llama. After learning this, I knew it was out of my hands, and we were getting married. If that's not fate, I don't know what is.

Emily you are so smart, so caring, and so hard working. You put so much of yourself into this celebration. Not a lot of you know this, but Emily was sick with a fever of 103 two days ago and looks absolutely stunning today. This week we had to physically stop her from helping put the finishing touches on today; that is how much she cared about making this the best celebration possible. Emily you are so incredible and so nice too. Emily's favorite comedian is herself, but occasionally I can get a laugh out of her. I enjoy making people smile and laugh but nothing gives me the satisfaction like making her laugh. I know when that happens, I have something good. I love getting her in goofy moods because that is when I am at my happiest as well.

A lot of people have mentioned how important Emily is to the Sheridan and Croghan family and how they would not function without her. I am the same way. I like staying active and playing sports, but as Tom mentioned I also like hanging on a couch with the shades pulled down and not seeing the light of day. With Emily that is impossible. She is always staying active and going on different adventures. My favorite adventure we did together was the day we got engaged. I have described it as the perfect Emily day. We started with an early workout class at Shred 415, which was life changing for Slimmy Jimmy here. From there we went on a nice bike ride through the city. We went to Sweet Greens, Pink Berry, and did the River Walk as well. Eventually we made our way to the grassy area outside the aquarium where I got down on one knee. I remember saying to her I am at my happiest when I am having days like this, and I want to spend the rest of my life having days like this with you. Today is another one of those days. Emily, I love you so much, and I cannot wait to spend the rest of my life having days like this with you forever.

My Father and Education

Education was very important to my father, Ed McCaskey. He had graduated from Saint Mary's School in Lancaster, Pennsylvania; Lancaster Catholic High School; and the University of Pennsylvania. Saint Mary's School and Catholic High helped to form my father as a good Catholic, husband, brother, father, uncle, and grandfather.

His great grandfather, John Piersol McCaskey, had been a great teacher and principal of Boys High School for over 50 years and then mayor of the town for two terms. He walked into the mayor's office because everybody who ever went to the high school carried a big coin with his picture. The inscription was "I am one of Jack's boys."

My father came in from grade school one day for lunch. His great grandfather said, "What did you learn in school today young man?"

My father said, "Nothing sir."

His great grandfather said, "Oh nothing. We must never have that. Fetch the Longfellow."

So that day, before my father got lunch, he learned that

"Lives of great men all remind us

We can make our lives sublime,

And, departing, leave behind us

Footprints on the sands of time."

J. P. McCaskey believed that education is a continuing process if we are to lead rich and fulfilling lives. At Catholic High my father learned to think and to utilize the talents that God gave him. He continued to expand and enjoy all that life has to offer.

On Thursday, June 2, 1988, my father was the commencement speaker at Catholic High. He said that receiving a diploma from Lancaster Catholic High School was one of the most important things that happened in his life.

My father had many conferences with his sons' teachers to encourage them to continue the good fight. He wrote notes to our teachers. "My son only got a D last quarter in your course. I think you're a better teacher than that, and so I'm going to give you another chance to prove yourself."

Walter McCaskey

My great-great uncle, Walter McCaskey, was born in Lancaster, Pennsylvania, on December 8, 1872. He was the fourth of seven children. He was a son of J. P. McCaskey and his wife, Ellen. Walter was a graduate of Boys' High School where his father was the principal.

For 2 years, Walter was on the Pennsylvania Nautical School Ship. He was capable of sailing a ship to any part of the world. He climbed ropes and furled sails. He excelled in boxing, wrestling, rowing, and swimming. When he was at Millersville Normal School, he learned the double trapeze act. He was absolutely honest and without fear.

When Walter was at Penn State, he won a prize in calculus and he was at the head of his class in mathematics. He was captain and quarterback of the football team in 1895. A game official wrote Walter "is as quick as lightning, a clean passer, a splendid tackler, and interferes finely."

Walter graduated with distinction in the special department of electrical engineering. He married Edna McClelland in 1899. He worked for the Pennsylvania Railroad in freight, steam-gauging, and draughting.

During the Spanish American War, he was a second lieutenant in the infantry in Manila. On a scouting mission, he saved one of his men from drowning.

After he had returned from the Philippines, he was stationed at Fort Yates and Fort Lincoln, near Bismarck, North Dakota. In 1918, he was a lieutenant colonel in France, serving as part of the American Expeditionary Force in World War I.

After the War, Walter and Edna resided in State College, Pennsylvania. He taught at Penn State. He retired from the Army as a colonel.

TUITION REBATE

For the last years of his life, Walter lived with my grandparents in Lancaster. I met him there in 1954 when I was five. He always wore a suit and a tie around the house.

Walter died on September 17, 1960, in Lancaster at the age of 86. He is buried at Arlington National Cemetery. My cousin, Phil McCaskey, has donated Walter's drinking cup and pocket watch to the Penn State Museum.

FACTS

To turn our dreams to a fact, it's up to you
Since we have the soul and the spirit
Never fear it, we'll see it through

—PKPMc

Some will argue that religious people ignore the facts and view the world as a fairy tale. They suggest that all Christians have ignored scientific discoveries and can't get themselves to believe in facts that most scientists accept.

Catholics like to point out that many of the important scientists have been great people of faith such as Georges Lemaïtre (1894-1966), a Belgian mathematician and Catholic priest who developed the theory of the Big Bang.[33] While the realm of supernatural exists outside the natural world, a scientist is no less scientific if he or she is a person of faith, just as a person of faith is no less faithful, if he or she is a scientist.

Yet, we are guided by our faith in the most significant ways. The work of science makes discoveries, but we have to make judgements about how to apply them. For my money, I would feel much more at ease with those making such judgements basing them on Judeo-

---

[33] Mark Midbon, "A Day Without Yesterday, George Lamaitre and the Big Bang," *Commonweal Magazine* Vol. 127 No. 6 (March 24, 2000) 18-19. Viewed at Catholic Education Resource Center, https://www.catholiceducation.org/en/science/faith-and-science/a-day-without-yesterday-georges-lemaitre-amp-the-big-bang.html on November 23, 2021.

Christian principles: life is sacred, love your neighbor, do not kill or steal—to name a few.

We know that Saint Thomas Aquinas worked to show that the principles of logic espoused by the great philosopher Aristotle could be used effectively not only in the way we view the natural world, but to some extent the Supernatural world. Faith and reason can coexist. Today, there are those who want to "defy logic" in the most fundamental ways. You can ignore logic or misinterpret logic, but humans can't defy logic.

The Curing of an Epileptic Boy
Mark 9:14-29

When Jesus and Peter and James and John
Came down from a high mountain, they came to
The other disciples and a great crowd.
When the crowd saw Jesus, they were amazed.

The father of an epileptic boy
Asked Christ to stop the seizures of his son.
The disciples were not able to help.
Christ invites the father to pray with faith.

Then Christ taught the disciples in private.
After His ascension, they had to pray.
Through the curing of an epileptic,
Christ teaches us to pray with confidence.

Mark Twain said, "I have the calm, quiet confidence of a Christian, with four aces."

Twenty-Four Birthday Questions

1. What are the Bears' Championship Seasons?
   1921, 1932, 1933, 1940, 1941, 1943, 1946, 1963, and 1985

2. What are the Bears' retired numbers and for whom? 3 Bronko Nagurski, 5 George McAfee, 7 George Halas, 28 Willie Galimore, 34 Walter Payton, 40 Gale Sayers, 41 Brian Piccolo, 42 Sid Luckman, 51 Dick Butkus, 56 Bill Hewitt, 61 Bill George, 66 Bulldog Turner, 77 Red Grange, 89 Mike Ditka

3. Which two Bears' players have had their numbers retired, but are not in the Pro Football Hall of Fame? 28 Willie Galimore and 41 Brian Piccolo

4. When was the white C first on the Bears' helmets? September 16, 1962

5. When was the orange C first on the Bears' helmets? September 16, 1973

6. Who are three first-round Chicago draft choices with the first name Kyle? Long, Fuller, and Schwarber

7. What did William Shakespeare's father say to William Shakespeare? Make plays

8. True or false: Martin Luther King Junior played quarterback for Morehouse College? True

9. Which 10 NFL coaches have won three or more NFL Championships? George Halas 6, Curly Lambeau 6, Bill Belichick 6, Vince Lombardi 5, Guy Chamberlin 4, Chuck Noll 4, Paul Brown 3, Weeb Ewbank 3, Joe Gibbs 3, and Bill Walsh 3

10. How many Bears have been elected to the Pro Football Hall of Fame? 30

11. Which Bear quarterbacks have played in the Pro Bowl? Johnny Lujack, Ed Brown, Bill Wade, Jim McMahon, and Mitch Trubisky

12. How many Bears have played in the Pro Bowl? 90

13. Where were you born?

14. Where did you grow up?

15. Where did you go to school?

16. Were you an athlete?

17. What was your best athletic accomplishment?

18. What did Charlotte write in her web? Some pig, terrific, radiant, and humble

19. Do you renounce Satan and all his empty promises?

20. What is your favorite birthday meal?

21. Which five NFL teams have won at least six Championships? Green Bay Packers 13, Chicago Bears 9, New York Giants 8, Pittsburgh Steelers 6, and New England Patriots 6

22. 93 Bears played Illinois high school football including seven Pro Football Hall of Famers. Who are the seven? Dick Butkus, Chicago Vocational; George Connor, Chicago De La Salle; Paddy Driscoll, Evanston; Red Grange, Wheaton; George Halas, Chicago Crane Tech; George Musso, Collinsville; George Trafton, Oak Park

23. In 1905, Teddy Roosevelt saved the game of football. He outlawed the flying wedge, and he encouraged more use of the forward pass. Would the game be further improved if we had to pass on every down?

24. In 1891, Jim Naismith invented the game of basketball. From 1891 through 1938, there was a center jump after every basket. From Seth Davis's biography of John Wooden (*Wooden: A Coach's Life*), we know that "Naismith viewed the center jump as akin to a kickoff in football. He worried that its elimination would allow too much scoring, and the fans would grow bored." We know that the elimination of the center jump after every basket improved the game of basketball. Would the elimination of the kickoff improve the game of football?

Sneakers Game

The Scots like to say there is no such thing as bad weather, only bad clothing.

The Bears looked unbeatable in 1934 when they went 13–0 for the season. Halas had added a new halfback, Beattie Feathers, who rushed for 1,004 yards that season. The Bears won 18-straight games and were dominating the league. The championship game on December 9, 1934, was a bizarre contest for the history books, or perhaps *Ripley's Believe It Or Not*. The Bears played the Giants in the Polo Grounds.[34]

The night before the game, a storm dumped freezing rain and sleet onto the field. Abe Cohen, who served part-time in the Giants' locker room and part-time in Manhattan College's locker room, was asked to head over to the school and borrow their basketball sneakers to help the Giants improve their footing. On icy field conditions, the Bears took a 13–3 lead before Cohen hopped out of a cab with a supply of basketball shoes.

At first, most of the Giants weren't sold on wearing sneakers. A few players wore them. But as the field conditions got worse, more of the Giants changed from cleats to sneakers. At some point in the game, the Giants became capable of outmaneuvering the Bears. The sneakered team scored 27 unanswered points for a 30–13 win.

Certainly, Halas was disappointed. He accepted the loss, but he vowed to make sneakers a part of every player's travel bag in the future.

Chicago Bears Alphabetically

Mike Adamle wrote poetry.
Dick Butkus was ubiquitous.
George Connor played with honor.
Mike Ditka really hit ya.

---

[34] Historic stadium of the New York Giants baseball team that was originally located in Central Park and later moved below a hill called Coogan's Bluff also in Manhattan about 6 miles away. The Giants football team played there as well through 1955.

Larry Ely was a happy guy.
Danny Fortmann had deportment.
Red Grange had great range.
George Halas inspired a palace.
Israel Idonije is the Bears' way
Stan Jones elicited groans.
Bob Kilcullen was not sullen.
Sid Luckman did not drive a truck man.
George McAfee played with glee.
Bronko Nagurski was not Chuck Swirsky.
Jim Osborne was not Keith Van Horne.
Walter Payton was a great sensation.
Robert Quinn helps us win.
Don Rives played without sleeves.
Mike Singletary was not contrary.
Bulldog Turner was a great learner.
Brian Urlacher was a great linebacker.
Keith Van Horne was not Jim Osborne.
Bill Wade led a championship parade.
My son, Tom, went to Xavier.
Maury Youmans is hard to rhyme.
Chris Zorich put quarterbacks in storage.

NFL Schedules

In the first decade of the NFL, the League was establishing itself and working out some consistency with the member teams and their schedules. At first, the number of games played varied from team-to-team. Teams formed and disbanded quickly. Of the inaugural season teams, only the Decatur Staleys/Chicago Bears and the Chicago/Saint Louis/Arizona Cardinals survived. Stronger markets were added and eventually the schedules were made consistent.

On September 24, 1933, the Bears opened the season with a 14–7 win over the Green Bay Packers. In 1933, the NFL went to a consistent 11-game schedule that would last until the war years.

On September 26, 1943, the Bears and Packers opened the 10-game season in a 21–21 tie. The War was taking its toll on the NFL and there were only eight active teams that year.

On September 29, 1946, the Bears opened the 11-game season with a 30–7 win over the Green Bay Packers. Sid Luckman was the Bears quarterback.

On September 28, 1947, the Bears would open the 12-game season losing to the Green Bay Packers, 29–20. The NFL would stick to a 12-game schedule until 1961.

On September 17, 1961, the Chicago Bears began their season by playing the Minnesota Vikings. The NFL regular schedule began a week earlier than the previous season as teams adjusted to their new 14-game regular season. It was the expansion-team Vikings first game of their inaugural season. They beat the Bears, 37–13, with Fran Tarkenton's 17 completions on 23 attempts for 250 yards and 4 touchdowns. Beating the Bears in the opener was a good first step for the franchise, but the Vikings would end up 3–13 for the season including a 52–35 loss to the Bears on December 17.

On September 3, 1978, the Chicago Bears began their first 16-game season by playing the Saint Louis Cardinals. The NFL regular schedule began 2 weeks earlier than the previous season as teams adjusted to the longer regular season. The Bears beat the Cardinals, 17–10. Bob Avellini was the Bears starting quarterback and Walter Payton and Roland Harper combined for 194 yards.

On September 12, 2021, the Chicago Bears began their first 17-game season by playing the Los Angeles Rams on Sunday night in Los Angeles. The Bears lost to the Rams, 34-14. The NFL regular schedule began on Thursday, September 9, 2021. The preseason was reduced to 3 games. To manage the uneven game schedule, teams will have nine home games and eight away games and vice versa the following year. Each team will continue to have one bye week.

Ed Sprinkle

Ed Sprinkle's image was newly minted in the Pro Football Hall of Fame in the 2020 Class. Sprinkle was described by George Halas as "the greatest pass rusher I've ever seen." Born in Bradshaw, Texas, Sprinkle grew up in Tuscola, Texas, played football at Hardin-Simmons University, then he transferred to the U.S. Naval Academy.

Once called "the meanest man in football," he played for the Bears from 1944-1955. Sprinkle was used as a blocker in his early years on the Bears. As he matured physically, he played right end on offense and defense, and then became a defensive specialist. Sprinkle was left-handed; this in addition to his quickness, speed off the ball, and his hyper aggressive play made him a difficult adversary.

Sprinkle once said on film, "I'd hit anybody on any play as hard as I could hit 'em and that's the way I played."[35] Coming off the end, he sometimes was able to reach over and make a close line tackle. That may have contributed to his reputation. Off the field, he was called a gentleman by many who knew him.

---

[35] Film shown at his induction (posthumously) into the Pro Football Hall of Fame.

Sprinkle was ahead of his time in that he was one of the first pass-rushing stars. The 4-time Pro Bowler was named to the Pro Football Hall of Fame All-1940s Team. Sprinkle played on the 1946 NFL Champion Bears. This Monster of the Midway is numbered among the Top 100 Bears of All Time.

Teaching and Coaching

When Vince Lombardi graduated from Fordham, he was not sure of what he wanted to do and employment was not easy to get. The Great Depression was still chugging along. In 1939, after a brief law school experience at Fordham and a few jobs that did not suit him, Lombardi took a position teaching at Saint Cecilia High School in Englewood, New Jersey.

At Saint Cecilia, Lombardi worked with Andy Palau, a former teammate of his at Fordham who was known as "Handy Andy" in his quarterback playing days. Lombardi served as Palau's assistant coach. Together they developed tremendous teams. And just as important, Lombardi was given a variety of teaching assignments. He would eventually spend most of his time on the sciences. For Lombardi, there would always be a connection between teaching and coaching.

Lombardi would move up to become head coach at Saint Cecilia before moving on to other coaching jobs.

STORIES

"I have always felt that the first duty of a writer was to ascend—to make flights, carrying others along if he could manage it."

—*E. B. White*

From Beowulf to the Waltons to Spider-Man, stories capture our imagination and teach us many things. It's hard to imagine a world without stories. The following explores my high school experiences in a fictional setting with life lessons and thoughts.

A Football Fairy Tale

Once upon a time there was a high school named Sports Faith. Its team was called the Apostles. It was located in the City of Sports Faith. Here is the list for summer reading.

Summer Reading List

Joan of Arc by Mark Twain
"If" by Rudyard Kipling
My Life and Hard Times by James Thurber
The Last Flower by James Thurber
The White Deer by James Thurber
Life with Father by Clarence Day Junior
One Man's Meat by E. B. White
The Wild Flag by E. B. White
The Trumpet of the Swan by E. B. White
Touchdown Pass by Clair Bee
A Pass and a Prayer by Clair Bee

Freshman Quarterback by Clair Bee
Ten Seconds to Play by Clair Bee
Fourth Down Showdown by Clair Bee
Triple Threat Trouble by Clair Bee
Fiery Fullback by Clair Bee
Champions in Sports and Spirit by Ed Fitzgerald
More Champions in Sports and Spirit by Ed Fitzgerald
Franny and Zooey by J. D. Salinger
The Homecoming by Earl Hamner Junior
Well, There's No Harm in Laughing by Frank Sullivan
The Last Catholic in America by John Powers
A River Runs Through It by Norman Maclean
Earth Works: Selected Essays by Scott Sanders
Markings by Seamus Heaney
From Values to Action by Harry Kraemer
Every Day Is Game Day: A 365-Day Sports Devotional by Pat Williams and Mark Atteberry
Home Waters: A Chronicle of Family and a River by John Maclean

Sports Faith Apostles

80 Thomas	Tom	Left End
77 Philip	Phil	Left Tackle
66 Bartholomew	Bart	Left Guard
54 James	Seamus	Center
61 Thaddaeus	Ted	Right Guard
74 Simon	Simon	Right Tackle
87 Andrew	Andy	Right End
10 Peter	Pete	Quarterback
24 James	Jim	Left Halfback
44 Matthew	Hew	Fullback
21 John	John	Right Halfback
20 Matthias	Matt	Kicker

Football Commandments

At the meeting with the parents and the players, Coach Francis, reviews five of his most important principles or Commandments of Football.

I. Football is a wonderful game. Be enthusiastic.

II. All previous games are preparation for the next one.

III. Obey the personal conduct policy.

IV. Work for the good of the team.

V. Win championships with sportsmanship.

After the last preseason practice, Team Chaplain Father Smyth said to Coach Francis, "You could always call it a rebuilding year."

Coach Francis said, "We've built."

Pep Rally

Pep rallies command the attention of everyone at Sports Faith High School. It's a great time to get the most important sports message across. At the school pep rally in the school gym before the first game, Father Smyth, the Team Chaplain, recites Sports Faith's football anthem with the students:

Bitterness is spiritual cancer.
Forgiveness is spiritual rapture.
Weather is a reminder that God is The Boss.
The Spirit strengthens us even after a loss.
Jesus Christ is The Man.
Salvation is The Plan.
When we dance God's dance,
He gives us another chance.
God's work is efficient.
His food is sufficient.

Here's a part of my prayers.
Coach and play without swears.

At the rally, Coach Francis puts everything into a
Christian perspective:

*"We want to win championships with sportsmanship.
We work diligently and we trust God for the results.
Like the Magi who followed the great star, we go
forward in faith.*

*"We are grateful that God created a wonderful world
in six days. Jesus died for sins, including fumbles.
When we need The Holy Spirit, He is there. He is even
there when we think that we don't need Him.*

*"We go to Mass and Bible Study and have daily
devotions. Our mandate is to love God and each other.
In our attempts to love, we are often funny.*

*"Sports Faith values its traditions. If we do not value
our opportunities and what was done in past, we are
not likely to work hard to preserve them.'*

The season

Football seasons come quickly once school starts. This
was a special season for Sports Faith High School.

On Friday, September 16, the Apostles played the
South Side Scribes at Sports Faith High School. It was
a beautiful fall night with cool air moving in during the
game. The stands were packed. Enthusiasm ran high.
Both teams demonstrated some nervous energy in the
first minutes of the game. With 6:05 left in the first
quarter, Jim, our left halfback, went in motion to the
right just before the snap. Quarterback Pete pivoted
left and handed off to Jim. The Apostles' offensive line

did not disappoint, they smashed a large hole in the defensive line which Jim followed up the middle for 52 yards and a touchdown. The crowd erupted with cheers. Matt kicked the extra point. Apostles 7–Scribes 0.

In the second quarter, the Apostles' possession had ground down to the Scribes 1. Nothing fancy was required. Hew, the Apostles' rugged fullback, took it up the middle for the score. After the extra point, the score was Apostles 14–Scribes 0.

After the half, the tension mounted as the Scribes were stopped on their side of the field and had to punt. The punt sailed high, the fans screamed, left halfback John caught the ball and returned the punt 67 yards straight up the right sideline to the 2. Jim ran it in from there. Matt kicked another extra point. The Apostles led, 21–0.

Ted squeezed in front of a Scribes' receiver and snagged an interception. Jim ran the final yard for yet another score. Another extra point—Apostles 28–Scribes 0.

In the fourth quarter, the Scribes were able to work up some excitement for their fans when they forced Pete to fumble, which was picked up, returned for 55 yards and a touchdown. The Apostles blocked the extra point attempt, Apostles 28–Scribes 6. The two teams battled to the end, but despite some desperate measures by the Saints, the final tally was Sports Faith 42–South Side Scribes 19.

On Friday, September 23, we played the O'Hare Pharisees at Sports Faith Stadium. Football was a great start to a wonderful weekend. Spirits were high to start, but the game went into the second half without a score.

It was another fall night with temps dropping from the low 70s into the 50s during the game.

Finally, in the third quarter, the Apostles moved close enough for Matt to kick a 20-yard field goal. The score was Apostles 3–Pharisees 0.

In the fourth quarter, excitement was in the air. After another possession for the Pharisees that ended in poor field position, they sent a punt our way that sailed end-over-end right onto our end of the field. Jim caught the punt with some distance between him and the rushing Saints. Tom threw himself at the Pharisees with a block that took two men out. Our excellent coaching was reflected when a wall of Apostles' blockers formed, and Jim was able to scamper down the left sideline for 64 yards. He was knocked out of bounds at the Pharisees 1. Hew was called on to take the ball up the middle for the score. Matt missed the extra point, wide right. The score was Apostles 9–Pharisees 0 and that is where it stood at the end. We felt lucky to leave with a win! The Pharisees had stymied our powerful offense, but we kept them out of the end zone all night.

On Friday, September 30, the Apostles were playing the Metro Catholic Romans at Sports Faith Stadium. The daytime temps were already about 10 degrees lower than the start of the season, but we got a decent dry evening although a little chilly. Sometimes the temps help sell a few hot chocolates at the concession stand. This was one of those nights. There was a little breeze as well.

In the first quarter, we pushed our way downfield with a series of passes and runs. Our offensive line was giving us time to pass and some running room. Hew ended our first drive with a 3-yard touchdown run. Matt kicked the extra point.

Our next series was a fan-pleaser. Our opposition tried to clog up the middle, but Pete flew around left end, avoiding all tacklers for 82 yards—touchdown! After Matt's extra point, it was Apostles 14–Romans 0.

Before we got too comfortable, the Romans responded with an excellent drive down the field. It ended with a quick 2-yard burst up the middle for a touchdown. After the extra point, we led 14–7.

The pressure was on, but we responded with another long drive that Hew finished off with a 2-yard touchdown run. On our last possession of the half, with ten seconds left, Pete faked a handoff at left tackle, rolled outside and ran 36 yards for another touchdown. Extra point good. Our lead was extended, Apostles 28–Romans 7.

In the second half, we continued to control the line of scrimmage and when the gun sounded, we won convincingly at 54–13.

On Saturday, October 8, we played the Saint Paul Corinthians away. It was their homecoming. It was our first day-game of the season and the temperature soared to 80 degrees. We felt the burn.

In the first quarter, Phil and Seamus busted through the line to pressure the quarterback just as he passed. Ted intercepted the floater and ran it back 46 yards for a touchdown. Matt delivered the extra point: Apostles 7–Corinthians–0.

The Corinthians came back in a hurry in the second quarter on an 80-yard run around left end for a touchdown. The game seemed to slow down. Neither team was finding much success on offense, but we finally closed in to field goal range and Matt put us ahead 10–7 with one through the uprights. We scored another touchdown in the fourth to make the final, 17–7.

On Friday, October 14, we played the Goose Island Galatians at Sports Faith Stadium. It was our homecoming. Another warm October evening with dry conditions and some wind gusts.

In the first quarter, the Galatians surprised us with a perfectly executed screen pass in the right flat that produced a 62-yard touchdown. It was the only time that the Apostles were behind all season, but the Galatians missed the point after. We countered with a long drive that our fullback Hew finished off with a 1-yard touchdown run. When Matt kicked the extra point, we were ahead, 7–6. We didn't want to get behind again and managed another drive that we finished off in crowd-pleasing fashion with right halfback John's 20 yard touchdown run. Matt kicked the extra point. Just before half we were in scoring position again and Hew took it in from 8 yards. We hungered for another victory. At the intermission, we were ahead 21–6.

Late in the third quarter, Seamus and Simon forced the Galatian QB to make a bad pass that Phil picked off and ran 38 yards for a touchdown. Matt missed the extra point. We scored once more before the gun, Apostles 34–Galatians 6. Tom had 2 interceptions. Hew had 10 tackles. Simon recovered a fumble on a punt.

On Friday, October 21, we played the North Shore Ephesians at Sports Faith Stadium. It was cold and windy. In the first quarter, at the end of a long drive, Pete faked a handoff to Hew off right tackle, rolled right, and threw an 11-yard touchdown pass to John. Matt kicked the extra point. On another possession, we decided to try it again. Pete faked to Hew off right tackle, rolled right, and threw a 19-yard touchdown pass to John. With the point after, we were ahead 14–0. In the second quarter, the Ephesians drove 53 yards for a score. Our lead was cut, 14–7. In the third quarter, Pete was back at it again, he faked to Hew off right tackle, rolled right, and threw a 43-yard touchdown pass to John. Matt kicked the extra point. The score was Apostles 21–Ephesians 7.

At the end of another drive, a play came in from the bench. Make it look like a pass, but Pete should run. Pete faked to Hew off right tackle, rolled right, faked a pass to John, and ran 24 yards for a touchdown. Matt kicked the extra point.

Our special teams came to play when Simon blocked a punt deep in Ephesians territory. Hew recovered it and ran 3 yards for a touchdown. Matt kicked the extra point. A couple more Apostles' touchdowns gave us a final of 49–7. Defense had some great numbers that game. Seamus had 18 tackles; Phil had 16; Andy had 15; Hew had 11; and Simon had 11.

On Sunday, October 30, we played the East End Philippians away. It was winter cold that day, but John warmed things up when he returned the opening kickoff 75 yards for a touchdown. Matt missed the extra point. Later in the quarter, with our first good drive of the day, Pete threw a 9-yard touchdown pass to the left end Tom. Matt kicked the extra point. We were ahead 13–0. The Philippians responded with a second quarter field goal, but they had problems covering the kick-off again when John returned it 47 yards to midfield. The Apostles drove down the field all the way to the 2 yard line where Pete executed a 2-yard quarterback sneak. Matt kicked the extra point. The score was Apostles 20–Philippians 3. The Philippians intercepted one of Pete's passes on the 30. They scored from there, but Andy blocked the extra point. The score was Apostles 20–Philippians 9. From there things got tough for the Philippians. For the Apostles, the second half highlight featured a little razzle-dazzle. John caught the opening kickoff and handed the ball off to Jim who ran it back 96 yards for the score! The Apostles won the game, 54–16.

On Friday, November 4, we played the DuPage Colossians away. It was a wintry night. It was a long drive to the home team's school way out west. In the first quarter, the Apostles had their way in the early moments of the game quickly driving down the field. Hew bulled his way into the end zone from 4-yards out. Matt's point-after gave the Apostles a quick 7–0 lead. Another possession, another Apostle touchdown, with Pete taking it up the middle on a quarterback sneak 5 yards for the score. Matt kicked the extra point. In the second quarter, Matt kicked a field goal making the Apostles tally at 17–0 at half.

In the third quarter, Hew was overpowering the Colossians defense. This time it was a 74 yard run for a touchdown. Matt kicked the extra point. The score was Apostles 24–Colossians 0. Pete dropped back and threw a 16-yard touchdown pass to Tom. Then John intercepted a wayward pass and ran 27 yards for yet another touchdown. Matt kicked the extra points and the score was Apostles 38–Colossians 0. Another touchdown from Hew ended the scoring and that's how the show ended. The Apostles had their 8th win in a row.

The score was Apostles 45–Colossians 0. Tom had 2 interceptions. Andy had 15 tackles. Simon blocked a punt. We did not punt at all in the game.

On Friday, November 11, we played the West Suburban Thessalonians at Apostles Stadium. Before the game, parents of the players lined up with their sons on the Apostles sideline and were introduced.

In the first quarter, after a long drive, Pete finished it off with a quarterback sneak for a yard and a touchdown. Matt kicked the extra point. The score was Apostles 7–Thessalonians 0.

The Thessalonians were having difficulty moving the ball and had to punt from the end zone. An errant snap was recovered by the punter in the end zone just as Hew tackled him for a safety. The score was Apostles 9–Thessalonians 0.

Working towards an undefeated season, Sports Faith was wasting no time. Another Apostles drive and the Apostles were inches away from another touchdown. Hew ran up the middle for a yard and a touchdown. Matt kicked the extra point. With 2 touchdowns and a safety, the score was Apostles 16–Thessalonians 0.

In the second quarter, the Thessalonian quarterback proved his mettle and ran for a touchdown. The snap on the extra point was bobbled. The score was Apostles 16–Thessalonians 6.

John ran up the middle and then down the right sideline 76 yards for a touchdown. Matt kicked the extra point. The score was Apostles 23–Thessalonians 6.

The Thessalonian quarterback dropped back, rolled right, and completed a pass to the running back at the Apostles 37; he ran down the right sideline for a touchdown. They missed the extra point to the right. The score was Apostles 23–Thessalonians–12.

With 25 seconds left in the half, Pete threw a 19-yard touchdown pass to Jim. Matt kicked the extra point. The score was Apostles 30–Thessalonians–12.

In the fourth quarter, Pete threw a 33-yard pass to Hew who ran the final 50 yards for a touchdown. Matt kicked the extra point. The score was Apostles 37–Thessalonians–12 and that's how it ended.

Andy had 12 tackles.

Sports Faith Apostles:
Football Schedule and Results

Friday, September 16	Scribes	Home	42–19
Friday, September 23	Pharisees	Home	9–0
Friday, September 30	Romans	Home	54–13
Saturday, October 8	Corinthians	Away	17–7
Friday, October 14	Galatians	Home	34–6
Friday, October 21	Ephesians	Home	49–7
Sunday, October 30	Philippians	Away	54–16
Friday, November 4	Colossians	Away	45–0
Friday, November 11	Thess.	Home	37–12

We were 9—0 and outscored our opponents 341–80. Our opponents did not score any points in the third quarter. The average score for each game was 38–9. It wasn't boring because we scored on offense, defense, and special teams. For the season, we had 30 rushing touchdowns, 10 passing touchdowns, 8 return touchdowns, 42 extra points, and 3 field goals.

We were only outscored in three quarters: the fourth quarter versus the Scribes, 19–14, and we won 42–19; in the second quarter at the Corinthians, 7–3, and we won 17–7; and the second quarter versus the Ephesians, 7–0, and we won 49–7.

Like John Wooden, Coach Francis wrote poetry. At the banquet, he shared his poem

"When"

When you strive and thrive for excellence rather
Than rationalize mediocrity
And can realize that you are no better than
Anyone else but certainly no worse,
When you know the sun will appear after an

TUITION REBATE

Eclipse and know that apathy is the
Opposite of love and not hate, and not be
Self-centered so you listen to others.

When you can dream positively and think
Actively so that you can assist friends
Rather than handicap them and be grateful
To the good God for your natural gifts,
When you can have people take you earnestly
Through a feeling of duty and a sense
Of humor and yet be unique and make your
Presence felt without being obnoxious.

When you maintain a belief in love and
Laughter rather than loneliness and tears,
When you stand in love rather than fall in it
And choose love gladly rather than madly,
When you need someone because you love her
Rather than love someone since you need her
When you have double cartwheels with only her
And have universal brotherly love,

When foes goad you into prudence rather than
Stupefy you into resignation,
When you are strong with faith in humanity
Rather than aggressive from fear of it,
When you maintain a belief in the last
Flower and the wild flag and also play
The trumpet of the swan to catch the white deer,
Then you'll be a great Sports Faith Apostle.

Apostles Retreat

The team went on a retreat together. Chaplain Father Smyth taught the team: "Remember the past with gratitude. Live the present with enthusiasm. Look to the future with confidence."

For the retreat, Parents are asked to write a letter for their son to open while the retreat is going on. Pete received a letter from his father.

Dear Son,

Now you are a high school senior and you are on your senior retreat. You are a very good student. You are on your way to a faith-based college where you will get an excellent education.

Most importantly, let's hope you're on your way to heaven. Regardless of where you go to college, let's keep the ultimate goal in mind. We're interested in schools that emphasize faith, education, and sports. We want to win championships with sportsmanship and we want to get to heaven. I'll be with you at the family retreat Mass.

It's important to grow physically, socially, culturally, and spiritually.

Physically, you are a very good athlete.

Socially, you are a very good family member and a very good friend.

Culturally, you are doing very well in school.

Spiritually, you go to Church and you exhibit sportsmanship. I want you to continue to be a servant leader like Jesus Who washed the feet of His Apostles. You are my beloved son in whom I am well pleased.

Jesus is my role model and I hope and trust that He is yours. Regardless of what others do, we need to do what is right.

We have God's grace and mercy that provide strength. Church and Bible Study and daily devotions keep us on the right path.

Your mother and I are praying that you will continue to grow in the Lord. If you are not called to the priesthood, I hope that you will marry a follower of Jesus, someone like your mother.

I enjoy being with you. You are very good company.

Pride is a sin. So I don't say that I am proud of you. I am grateful that you are my son. Thank you. I love you. It's great to be with you.

Your earthly father,

Sports Faith Sportsmanship Award

On Pentecost Vigil, Pete received the Sports Faith Sportsmanship Award. Here is his acceptance speech.

"Thank you very much. It's an honor to be here this evening and receive this award.

"I think it's important to develop physically, socially, culturally, and spiritually. Physically, I have the opportunity to play football and run track for Sports Faith High School. Socially, I have a date for the prom, but we won't be going to the picnic the next day because I have the district track meet. Culturally, I read an essay that wasn't even assigned: "University Days" by James Thurber. I write essays and poems about sports and faith for my school literary magazine. Spiritually, at Sports Faith High School, we can go to Mass and Communion every day.

"*The Bible says that to whom much is given, much is expected. Money will go to my favorite charity, Sports Faith International.*

"*I thank God for my family, my friends, my coaches, my teachers, and my teammates. God has been very, very good to me.*

Walk-a-Thon Dons

We who have dreams, when we walk, they'll come true.
To turn our dreams, to a fact, is up to you.
If you have the soul and the spirit
Never fear, it will see you through.
Hearts may inspire
Other hearts with their fire
For the strong obey
When God Almighty shows us the way.

God give us Dons
Who are God-fearing Dons
Who will walk for the school they adore.

Start us with seven
Who are God-fearing Dons
And we'll soon have
Seven hundred more

Shoulder to shoulder
And bolder and bolder
We grow as we go to the fore
Then there's nothing in the world
Can halt or mar a plan
When God-fearing Dons,
Can walk together like we can.

The Way of the Cross Rescued Us from Loss

Jesus was condemned. We have hope to lend.
Jesus took up His Cross. We don't have a loss.
Jesus Christ fell. We have been saved from Hell.
Christ met His mother. We love each other.

Simon helped Jesus. We help to please us.
Veronica helped Jesus. Don't tease us.
Jesus fell again. We rise before ten.
Jesus consoled the women. We are men.

The third fall. To get to Church do not stall.
Jesus Christ was stripped. We do not get clipped.
Jesus was crucified. We have not died.
Jesus died. We have not been crucified.

Jesus was taken down. We get a crown.
Jesus was buried. Our sins are carried.

Birth Dates and Death Dates of Writers

January 1, 1919	J. D. Salinger was born.
January 2, 1928	L. E. Sissman was born.
January 6, 1878	Carl Sandburg was born.
January 7, 1940	Ira Berkow was born.
January 10, 1943	Jim Croce was born.
January 15, 1982	Red Smith died.
January 17, 2013	John Powers died.
January 27, 2010	J. D. Salinger died.
February 3, 1907	James Michener was born.
February 12, 1809	Abraham Lincoln was born.
February 19, 1976	Frank Sullivan died.
March 1, 1921	Richard Wilbur was born.

March 2, 1859	Shalom Aleichem was born.
March 2, 1896	Clair Bee was born.
March 4, 2016	Pat Conroy died.
March 6, 1885	Ring Lardner was born.
March 10, 1976	L. E. Sissman died.
March 17, 1956	Fred Allen died.
March 24, 2016	Earl Hamner Junior died.
April 1, 2008	Arturo Vivante died.
April 6, 1935	Edwin Arlington Robinson died.
April 13, 1939	Seamus Heaney was born.
April 15, 1865	Abraham Lincoln died.
April 17, 1897	Thornton Wilder was born.
April 18, 1945	Ernie Pyle died.
April 21, 1910	Mark Twain died.
April 23, 1616	William Shakespeare died.
April 24, 1905	Robert Penn Warren was born.
May 3, 1924	Yehuda Amichai was born.
May 3, 1940	Pat Williams was born.
May 6, 1862	Henry David Thoreau died.
May 6, 1919	L. Frank Baum died.
May 8, 1895	Bishop Sheen was born.
May 13, 1916	Shalom Aleichem died.
May 15, 1856	L. Frank Baum was born.
May 15, 1886	Emily Dickinson died.
May 16, 1955	James Agee died.
May 17, 2019	Herman Wouk died.
May 19, 1971	Ogden Nash died.
May 20, 1908	Jimmy Stewart was born.
May 20, 1983	Clair Bee died.
May 27, 1915	Herman Wouk was born.

May 30, 2007	Mark Harris died.
May 31, 1894	Fred Allen was born.
June 4, 2010	John Wooden died.
June 8, 1889	Gerard Manley Hopkins died.
June 15, 2017	Bill Dana died.
June 28, 2014	Jim Brosnan died.
July 2, 1997	Jimmy Stewart died.
July 10, 1923	Earl Hamner Junior was born.
July 11, 1899	E. B. White was born.
July 12, 1817	Henry David Thoreau was born.
July 12, 1895	Oscar Hammerstein II was born.
July 21, 1933	John Gardner was born.
July 22, 1967	Carl Sandburg died.
July 24, 1874	Oswald Chambers was born.
July 28, 1844	Gerard Manley Hopkins was born.
July 29, 1878	Don Marquis was born.
August 2, 1990	Norman Maclean died.
August 3, 1900	Ernie Pyle was born.
August 7, 1942	Garrison Keillor was born.
August 15, 1935	Will Rogers died.
August 19, 1902	Ogden Nash was born.
August 23, 1884	Will Cuppy was born.
August 23, 1960	Oscar Hammerstein II died.
August 30, 2013	Seamus Heaney died.

September 5, 1929   Bob Newhart was born.
September 14, 1982   John Gardner died.
September 15, 1889   Robert Benchley was born.
September 15, 1989   Robert Penn Warren died.
September 19, 1935   J. P. McCaskey died.
September 19, 1949   Will Cuppy died.
September 20, 1973   Jim Croce died.
September 22, 1892   Frank Sullivan was born.
September 22, 2000   Yehuda Amichai died.
September 25, 1905   Red Smith was born.
September 25, 1933   Ring Lardner died.
September 28, 1935   Bob Schul was born.

October 1, 1985   E. B. White died.
October 5, 1924   Bill Dana was born.
October 9, 1837   J. P. McCaskey was born.
October 14, 1910   John Wooden was born.
October 14, 2017   Richard Wilbur died.
October 16, 1997   James Michener died.
October 17, 1923   Arturo Vivante was born.
October 24, 1929   Jim Brosnan was born.
October 25, 1400   Geoffrey Chaucer died.
October 26, 1945   Pat Conroy was born.
October 26, 1945   Scott Sanders was born.

November 2, 1961   James Thurber died.
November 4, 1897   Will Rogers was born.
November 4, 1949   Philip Yancey was born.
November 15, 1917   Oswald Chambers died.
November 18, 1874   Clarence Day Junior was born.
November 19, 1922   Mark Harris was born.
November 21, 1945   Robert Benchley died.
November 22, 1899   Hoagy Carmichael was born.

November 22, 1963	C. S. Lewis died.
November 27, 1909	James Agee was born.
November 29, 1898	C. S. Lewis was born.
November 30, 1835	Mark Twain was born.
November 30, 1945	John Powers was born.
November 30, 1983	Richard Llewellyn died.
December 7, 1975	Thornton Wilder died.
December 8, 1894	James Thurber was born.
December 8, 1906	Richard Llewellyn was born.
December 9, 1979	Bishop Sheen died.
December 10, 1830	Emily Dickinson was born.
December 22, 1869	Edwin Arlington Robinson was born.
December 23, 1902	Norman Maclean was born.
December 27, 1981	Hoagy Carmichael died.
December 28, 1935	Clarence Day Junior died.
December 29, 1937	Don Marquis died.
December 30, 1937	Paul Stookey was born.
December 31, 1965	Nicholas Sparks was born.

COACHES

"Good coaching may be defined as the development of character, personality and habits of players, plus the teaching of fundamentals and team play."

–Clair Bee

In 2014, I published a book with Sporting Chance Press called *Pillars of the NFL: Coaches Who Have Won Three or More Championships.* The book describes the football lives of George Halas, Guy Chamberlin, Curly Lambeau, Paul Brown, Weeb Ewbank, Vince Lombardi, Chuck Noll, Bill Walsh, Joe Gibbs, and Bill Belichick. These most successful coaches had a wide range of personalities, practices, and strategies. Yet, reading about their lives can help us understand what led to success in one of the most difficult environments imaginable. Here are highlights of their efforts.

George Halas

George Halas coached for 40 seasons and holds an overall NFL head-coaching record of 324–151–31. The Bears won six NFL Championships with Halas as coach and a total of eight as NFL owner. Halas was present at the beginning of the NFL and worked tirelessly for over 60 years to see professional football succeed. Halas was named AP Coach of the Year, the Sporting News Coach of the Year, and the UPI NFL Coach of the Year for both 1963 and 1965. He was enshrined in Pro Football Hall of Fame's charter class of 1963.

If anyone could be called the Father of the NFL, it would be George Halas. In this way, his nickname, Papa Bear says it all. Halas and a small group of men developed the framework for professional football in the humblest circumstances—a meeting in a car showroom in Canton, Ohio. It took decades to make it work. No one worked as hard or as long as George Halas.

No one had as big a stake in the game as George Halas. He was a leader who enjoyed the game and loved players who were tough that gave the game everything they had. Halas certainly gave the game everything that he had. No one had more "skin in the game" than Halas. Success was survival—something not many understand in the 21st century.

Guy Chamberlin

Guy Chamberlin was a farm boy from Nebraska. An intense competitor, Chamberlin liked to say that no one ever loved the game more than him. His winning ways earned him the nickname, "Champ."

Chamberlin coached from 1922-1927. He played during that time as well, but little in 1927. He won four championships. Prior to his coaching career, he played for George Halas and the Decatur-Chicago Staleys in 1920-1921. The Staleys won the Championship in 1921. In 8 years, Chamberlin was a part of five championship teams. Chamberlin holds an overall NFL head-coaching record of 58-16-7.

A game-changer, Chamberlin's play was inextricably woven into his total contribution to the game over his career. When he was winning championships, he was winning them on the field as a player as well as a coach. Chamberlin was a powerful athlete who Jim Thorpe and George Halas befriended in his early career. Champ was one of the earliest successes in professional football. He never thought professional football would last and he left the game after 8 years. None of the teams Chamberlin coached to championships has survived. A University of Nebraska award is named for Chamberlin, but in pro football history his name was little known until recently.[36]

Chamberlin's success was astounding. His tremendous success in less than a decade was all but forgotten as we entered the 21st century.

Curly Lambeau

Curly Lambeau won six NFL championships including three in a row, 1929-1931. In 33 years of coaching, he holds an overall NFL head-coaching record of 226–132 –22. He developed the only successful surviving NFL franchise in a small market. He was one of the few highly successful player-coaches in the NFL and he was one of the earliest promoters of the passing game. His Packers were perhaps the greatest David and Goliath story in sports history.

Curly Lambeau became an international celebrity and advocate for professional football throughout the world. Loving this leading role, he sometimes spent the offseason in Hollywood. Enshrined in the charter class of 17 members in the Pro Football Hall of Fame in 1963, he holds the NFL's fourth highest win total in the 20th century. In his honor, the Green Bay Packers fittingly christened their stadium Lambeau Field on September 11, 1965, following the coach's death the previous June.

Lambeau was a superb athlete and judge of talent. He never lost confidence in himself although early in his

---

[36] Sporting Chance Press's *Pillars of the NFL* and its related research and publication efforts have helped to call attention to Guy Chamberlin and his contributions to the game. Some of the more publicized events around football history and the 100 year anniversary of the NFL have also increased an interest in the past and a look at the greats.

career some of his players seemed to have a better understanding of the game. He worked with a network of community leaders and citizens who made sacrifices to keep the little town team alive. Lambeau was an exuberant coach, competitor, and administrator.

Paul Brown

Paul Brown's Cleveland teams won four AAFC titles and three NFL crowns while competing in ten consecutive championship games.[37] Brown had only one losing season at Cleveland in 17 years. In Cincinnati, where Brown started up the Bengals under a highly restrictive expansion draft, his team was atop the AFC Central Division in its third year. The Bengals were atop their division in 1973 and in Brown's last season in 1975. Brown holds an overall NFL/AAFC head coaching-record of 222–112–9.

The only coach to have an NFL team named after him, Brown was inducted into the Pro Football Hall of Fame in 1967. Massillon's Tiger Stadium was renamed Paul Brown Tiger Stadium in honor of the coach in 1976. The home of the Cincinnati Bengals, which opened in 2000, was also named Paul Brown Stadium. At Miami University where Brown played, he is honored with a statue, the ninth one in the "Cradle of Coaches" Plaza that calls attention to the highly successful coaches with Miami roots. Brown was named Sporting News NFL Coach of the Year for 1951 and 1953. He was named UPI

---

[37] The AAFC was the All-American Football Conference, a professional football league that operated from 1946-1949 to challenge the National Football League. The AAFC was short-lived, but after the league folded, Brown's Cleveland Browns team along with the San Francisco 49ers were folded into the NFL. A third team, the original Baltimore Colts was also added to the NFL, but that team only survived one season after its entry.

NFL Coach of the Year for 1957; UPI AFL Coach of the Year for 1969 and 1970.

Brown was disciplined in teaching football skills and knowledge. He focused on classroom work for each season start, playbooks before they were in vogue, and practices that were strictly scheduled from beginning to end. He wanted only intelligent players of good character.

Weeb Ewbank

The indefatigable Weeb Ewbank was the only coach to win championships in both the AFL and the NFL.[38] He was a tremendous team-builder who took two fledgling teams, the Baltimore Colts and the New York Jets, to the pinnacle of professional football success. Ewbank holds an overall NFL head-coaching record of 134–130–7. He won three NFL Championships including one Super Bowl victory.

Ewbank successfully coached two of the most talented quarterbacks of their time: Johnny Unitas and Joe Namath. Ewbank's first Colts' Championship win in 1958 went into sudden death overtime and it is considered a game that won over millions of fans to the NFL.

When his Jets beat the Colts in Super Bowl III, the game was another blockbuster event for a different reason. It was the compelling story of the upstart Jets of

---

[38] The American Football League (AFL) was another competing league in professional football that operated from 1960 until 1970. In a 1966 agreement, both leagues agreed to a merger that was to be consummated in 1970. But from 1967, both leagues sent their championship teams to compete in a common championship game that would eventually be dubbed the Super Bowl. When the teams of both leagues were merged, two NFL conferences were formed: the American Football Conference and the National Football Conference.

the AFL defeating the mighty Colts. Ewbank was named UPI NFL Coach of the Year for 1958. He was inducted into the Pro Football Hall of Fame in 1978.

Although Ewbank, like other NFL coaches, was constantly under tremendous pressure, he was physically, mentally, and emotionally sturdy. Ewbank negotiated salaries with his players and regardless of how unreasonable talks might become, he maintained the positive outlook of a man who always enjoyed life. Ewbank lived for 91 years.

Vince Lombardi

Vince Lombardi won five NFL championships in 9 years including the first two Super Bowl crowns. His three championships in a row matches the accomplishment of Curly Lambeau and Guy Chamberlin. He holds an overall NFL head-coaching record of 105–35–6. Lombardi was named both the AP and UPI NFL Coach of the Year for 1959 and the Sporting News Coach of the year for 1961. He was inducted into the Pro Football Hall of Fame posthumously with the Class of 1971. The Super Bowl trophy is named the "Lombardi Trophy" in his honor.

Lombardi combined the discipline of Colonel Blaik of West Point with the motivational skills of Knute Rockne of Notre Dame in a time when many people thought that the world was too cynical for either of them. Under Lombardi's philosophy, by working to excel at football, a football player excels at life—he seeks to achieve his potential. For Lombardi, football was not a metaphor for life, it was an integral part of it—not just for him, but for his players and fans.

Lombardi was winning championships with discipline and hard work at a time when society was all about protest and rebellion. Did Lombardi have the best talent to win five Championships or did he drill his players into believing that they were the best prepared and could overcome the odds? Lombardi was persuasive and extremely hard working.

Chuck Noll

Chuck Noll's Steelers won four Super Bowls in 6 years and nine AFC Central Division Championships. Over his 23 seasons as head coach of the Steelers, Noll holds an overall NFL head-coaching record of 209–156–1. Noll received the inaugural Earle "Greasy" Neale Award for Professional Coach of the Year from the Maxwell Football Club. He was named the UPI Coach of the Year in 1972. He was inducted into the Pro Football Hall of Fame in 1993.

Noll was pro football's 1970s answer to the winning traditions of Paul Brown and Vince Lombardi. He was organized and focused on teaching like Brown. He wanted his players to be just as disciplined as Brown's men of the late 1940s and 1950s. Noll pushed his Steelers to be fierce like Lombardi's Packers, but he wanted those qualities to be lasting and come from within.

Noll was not the consummate motivator like Lombardi, but he focused on getting a few of the right players like Joe Greene who could motivate the rest of the team to be champions. The Steelers went from a poor performing franchise to one that won Championships and produced Hall of Fame players.

Bill Walsh

Bill Walsh coached the San Francisco 49ers from 1979-1988 and posted a 102-63-1 record including Super

Bowl victories in XVI, XIX, and XXIII. Walsh created the NFL's Minority Coaches Internship and Outreach Program to help foster the advancement and success of minority coaches. Walsh was inducted into the Pro Football Hall of Fame in 1993 and he was named the AP, UPI, Sporting News, and Pro Football Weekly NFL Coach of the Year in 1981 and the UPI NFL Coach of the Year in 1984.

Walsh also had an eye for talent that focused on what athletes could do and make them more confident and consistent in those efforts. Walsh developed several excellent quarterbacks—work that was coupled with a strategy to spread the field using a more calculated passing game. Borrowing on other innovative offensive-minded strategies that used the pass liberally, he developed what is called the West Coast Offense. Walsh was also intense, determined, and competitive.

Walsh questioned himself at times, but he always had confidence in his view that the quarterback position was key. He believed that he could help an inconsistent but talented quarterback become a consistent performer. When he drafted Joe Montana, he was determined to see his vision carried out. Under the watchful and relentless eye of Walsh, Montana excelled. Meanwhile Walsh built a world-class team around his quarterback.

Joe Gibbs

In Gibbs's first 12-season stretch as the Washington Redskins' coach, he led his team to three Super Bowl victories and four NFC Championships. His Redskins made the playoffs an incredible eight times in 12 years. His .683 winning percentage was third best behind Vince Lombardi and John Madden. Gibbs holds an overall NFL head-coaching record of 171–101–0. Gibbs was enshrined in the Pro Football Hall of Fame in 1996.

He was named AP Coach of the Year in 1982 and 1983; Sporting News Coach of the Year in 1982, 1983, and 1991; Pro Football Weekly Coach of the Year in 1982 and 1983; and UPI Coach of the Year in 1991.

Gibbs took stock of his talent and put together a program to win that was based on existing personnel. His high-energy, tireless approach to creating game plans consumed long hours well into the night, but the effort was visible on the playing field. And regardless of his lofty success, Gibbs always respected and appreciated his players, his coaches, his fans, and his owners.

Bill Belichick

The NFL game today is a mix of physicality and strategic planning and implementation. Professional football includes heady plans and preparations that put a premium on brain power. There are preseason strategies, pregame strategies, second half "adjustments," and postseason strategies. Bill Belichick is a master strategist in all categories. He is also a life-long learner.

Bill Belichick brings military discipline into his coaching program to build teams that are consistently among the top in the NFL. His overall NFL record is 321–156–0 through the 2021 season. He has six NFL championships to his credit—winning Super Bowl XXXVI, Super Bowl XXXVIII, Super Bowl XXXIX, Super Bowl XLIX, Super Bowl LI, and Super Bowl LIII—and he has nine AFC Championships.

Belichick was named AP Coach of the Year in 2003, 2007, and 2010; Sporting News Coach of the Year in

2003 and 2007; and Pro Football Weekly Coach of the Year in 2003 and 2007.

Belichick's coaching decisions demonstrate a complete understanding of the game in every phase. His program consistently develops player skills that counter opposition strengths. Players predict opposition moves and understand the reasoning behind them. Unselfish players "do their job" and fill in for others. The right personnel move overrides any emotional attachment.

Area of Studies Reading Room, Library of Congress

BOOKS

My parents were members of the greatest generation and they believed in education and reading.

Too Busy to Read

An hour with a book would have brought to his mind
The secret that took him a whole year to find
The facts that he learned at enormous expense
Were all on a library shelf to commence.
Alas! for our hero; too busy to read,
He was also too busy, it proved, to succeed.
We may win without credit or backing or style,
We may win without energy, skill or a smile,
Without patience or aptitude, purpose or wit—
We may even succeed if we're lacking in grit;
But take it from me as a mighty safe hint—
A civilized man cannot win without print.

—Anonymous

Updated Champions in Sports and Spirit

When I was a child, there was a series of books called Vision Books. They were about saints and other wonderful people. My parents gave us these books for ourselves and for our friends when we were invited to their birthday parties.

My two favorite books in this series were *Champions in Sports and Spirit* and *More Champions in Sports and Spirit.*

Ed Fitzgerald

Ed Fitzgerald wrote the *Champions in Sports and Spirit* Series. The first book was published in 1956. The second book was published in 1959. This chapter completes the story of the great athletes in Fitzgerald's books.

Ed Fitzgerald was born on September 10, 1919, in the Bronx, New York City. When he was in high school, he wrote about high school sports for the city's newspapers. During World War II, he served in the Army. In 1946, he started as a writer and an editor for *Sport* magazine. In 1951, he became the editor.

From 1960 through 1968, Fitzgerald was president of the Doubleday books division. Then he was president of McCall's Magazine Group. From 1973 through his retirement in 1984, he was president of the Book-of-the-Month Club.

Fitzgerald and his wife, Libuse, had one son, Kevin; one daughter, Eileen; and one granddaughter, Leona. He died of a stroke on February 11, 2001 in New Rochelle, New York at the age of 81.

He was the author of many books, including biographies of Mickey Mantle, Johnny Unitas, and Yogi Berra. He was the editor of the autobiography of Althea Gibson.

Fitzgerald's memoirs are *A Nickel an Inch* and *That Place in Minnesota.*

Champions in Sports and Spirit was about Gil Hodges, Rocky Marciano, Maureen Connolly, Maurice Richard, Bob Cousy, Terry Brennan, and Yogi Berra. *More Champions in Sports and Spirit* was about Stan

TUITION REBATE

Musial, Carmen Basilio, Alex Olmedo, Juan Manuel Fangio, Ron Delany, Eddie Arcaro, Jean Beliveau, and Herb Score.

Gil Hodges

Gil Hodges was born April 4, 1924 in Princeton, Indiana. He was a three-sport athlete (football, basketball, and track) at Petersburg High School. He played American Legion baseball. He was a four-sport athlete (football, basketball, baseball, and track) at Saint Joseph's College in Rensselaer, Indiana. During World War II, he served in the Marine Corps. In 1946, he played catcher for the Newport News Dodgers. In 1947, he played first base for the Brooklyn Dodgers.

From 1947-1961, he played for the Brooklyn/Los Angeles Dodgers. From 1962-1963, he played for the New York Mets. He was 6-foot-1½; he weighed just over 200 pounds. From 1963-1967, he was the manager of the Washington Senators. From 1968-1971, he was the manager of the New York Mets.

Hodges was an eight-time All-Star (1949-1955, 1957), a three-time World Series Champion (1955, 1959, 1969), and a three-time Gold Glove Award winner (1957-1959).

In the spring of 1948, he met his wife, Joan, at a party that his landlady had given. For their first date, they went to see the movie, "The Bells of Saint Mary's" with Bing Crosby as Father O'Malley. They got married on December 26, 1948 at Saint Gregory's Church in Brooklyn. They had one son: Gil Junior; and three daughters: Irene, Cynthia, and Barbara.

Hodges was well-known as a devout Catholic. When he was in a slump, fans sent him letters and good-luck gifts. Father Herbert Redmond of Saint Francis Xavier

167

Church in Brooklyn said, "It's too warm for a sermon. Go home, keep the Commandments—and say a prayer for Gil Hodges." The slump eventually ended.

Hodges was polite and respectable to umpires. After he had hit a home run, as he crossed the plate, he blew a kiss to his wife. On August 31, 1950, he hit four home runs in one game. In January 1955, the New York Press Photographers Association named Hodges and Stan Musial as the most cooperative athletes in the world of sports.

On Easter Sunday, April 2, 1972, Hodges died of a heart attack in West Palm Beach, Florida, at the age of 47. Yogi Berra succeeded Hodges as the manager of the New York Mets. Ray McKenna and Catholic Athletes for Christ made a video to help Gil Hodges get elected to the National Baseball Hall of Fame for induction in 2022.[39]

Rocky Marciano

Rocky Marciano's parents were immigrants from Italy. He was born September 1, 1924, in Brockton, Massachusetts. He had two brothers, Louis and Peter, and three sisters, Alice, Concetta, and Elizabeth.

When Rocky was 2 years old, he almost died of pneumonia. He was a Sunday-school pupil at Saint Patrick's Parochial School in Brockton. He was a three-sport athlete (football, wrestling, and baseball) for Brockton High School. After his sophomore year, he worked for the Brockton Ice and Coach Company. He was also a ditch digger, a railroad layer, and a shoemaker. He lived in Hanson, Massachusetts.

---

[39] The film is called Soul of a Champion: The Gil Hodges Story. See the official website: https://www.gilhodgesfilm.com/

TUITION REBATE

During World War II, Marciano served in the Army. He went out for the baseball team and volunteered for the camp boxing matches. This helped him get out of washing dishes. While he was awaiting his discharge, he continued boxing.

In March 1947, Marciano tried out for the Fayetteville, North Carolina Cubs, but he did not make the team. Then he returned to Brockton; he helped clear land with a pick and a shovel. He also took up amateur boxing. At the age of 23, he took up professional boxing.

Marciano was 5-foot-10½. On July 12, 1948, he had his first professional fight in Princeton, New Jersey. He had 49 professional fights and he won all of them. On September 23, 1952, he became the heavyweight champion. He retired on April 27, 1956.

Marciano was modest and unassuming. He carried himself with quiet dignity. He didn't drink or smoke. He went to church at Saint Colman's Parish. He practiced what he preached to the youth; he was a dedicated athlete. He ran five miles before lunch; he always tried to make himself a better boxer.

After he had retired from boxing, he hosted a weekly boxing television show. He was a wrestling referee. He was a businessman. He lived in Wilton Manors, Florida, a suburb of Fort Lauderdale.

Marciano was a serious Catholic. He and his wife, Barbara, had a daughter, Mary Anne, and a son, Rocco Kevin. Rocky died on August 31, 1969 at the age of 45 in a small private plane crash in Newton, Iowa. His 46th birthday was the next day.

Mo Connolly

Maureen Catherine "Mo" Connolly was born September 17, 1934, in San Diego. She earned tennis lessons by being a ball-chaser.

At the beginning of her career, Maureen switched from being a left-handed player to being a right-handed player. She was 5-foot-5 and weighed 130 pounds. Her favorite singers were Bing Crosby and Gordon MacRae.

Maureen was a devout Catholic. She went to parochial schools and she graduated from Cathedral High School in San Diego. She was a B student. In September 1951, she won the U.S. Championship (in Tennis—now known as the U.S. Open).[40] When she returned to San Diego, she received a present paid for by small contributions from people from all over the city. It was a saddle horse named Colonel Merryboy.

Shortly after that, Maureen met Norman Brinker. He had ridden with the U.S. Equestrian Team in the 1952 Olympic Games in Helsinki. He was 21 and she was 18. She interviewed him for a column she wrote in the *San Diego Union*. She quickly found out that he was not married or engaged.

In 1953, Maureen won Wimbledon, the U. S. Championship, the Australian Championship, and the French Championship. From 1951 through 1953, she was the Associated Press Female Athlete of the Year. In 1954, she won the French Championship and Wimbledon.

In February 1955, she announced in her column that she was retiring from tennis. She also announced her engagement to Norman.

---

[40] Tennis championships moved to abolish the line between amateurs and pros in Open tournaments.

On June 11, 1955, they got married at Saint Patrick's Church in San Diego. It was the parish in which she had been born. Bishop Charles Buddy was the celebrant. He said, "You have chosen the better part to become the queen of a home instead of queen of the courts."

Norman & Maureen had two daughters, Cindy and Brenda. Maureen wrote for U. S. and British newspapers at major U. S. tennis tournaments. She also coached tennis and established a foundation to promote junior tennis.

In 1966, Maureen was diagnosed with ovarian cancer. She died on June 21, 1969 in Dallas, Texas, at the age of 34.[41]

Maurice Richard

Maurice Richard was born on August 4, 1921 in Montreal, Quebec. He was the oldest of eight children. He had three sisters: Georgette, Rollande, and Marguerite. He had four brothers: Rene, Jacques, Henri, and Claude.

When he was 14, he started playing organized hockey. He also played baseball and he was a boxer. When he was 16, he went to technical school to become a machinist. When he was 17, he met his future wife, Lucille Norchet; she was almost 14. On September 12, 1942, they got married. He was 21; she was 17. They had seven children: Hugette, Maurice Junior, Normand, Andre, Suzanne, Polo, and Jean; and 14 grandchildren.

In the winter of 1941, Maurice knocked on the door of the Montreal Canadiens and he said, "I want to play

---

[41] Connolly's husband, Norman Brinker, went on to establish several restaurant chains and many new restaurant industry concepts.

hockey." He was given a tryout and then he was sent to the minor leagues.

From Ed Fitzgerald, we know that, "The Catholic background of most of the players and fans is reflected in the Latin motto which hangs in the Canadiens' dressing room: Celeritas—Auctoritas—Aeternaque. It means Speed—Authority—Eternally, and it was suggested by a Catholic priest who followed the team enthusiastically.

"The religious training of the players is also shown in their devotion to the game and to the all-important principles of training. An outsider once observed that the Canadiens' locker room has the refined atmosphere of a choirboys' cloakroom. It was an apt remark. You will never see a cigarette butt or a beer can in there; none of the players smokes or drinks in the dressing room. Most of them don't smoke or drink anywhere. They feel that it is no sacrifice if it helps them play better hockey."

From 1942-1960, Maurice played wing for the Canadiens. He was 5-foot-10; he weighed 180 pounds. In 1947, he was the National Hockey League Most Valuable Player. He was on eight championship teams. He was an all-star 14 times. For the last 5 years of his playing career, the Canadiens won five championships. The teams had basically the same 12 players. They were nicknamed the 12 Apostles.

After he had stopped playing, he was an ambassador for the Canadiens and he was a businessman. He is a Hockey Hall of Famer.

In 1994, Lucille died of cancer. In 1998, Maurice was diagnosed with abdominal cancer. He died on May 27, 2000 in Montreal at the age of 78.

Bob Cousy

Bob Cousy was born August 9, 1928 in Manhattan, New York. He played basketball for Saint Pascal's Elementary School and Andrew Jackson High School in Queens, New York. In the summer before college, he worked as a waiter in a hotel resort in the Catskills. In the evenings there, he played basketball.

Bob was a three-time All American for Holy Cross College in Worcester, Massachusetts. He received Holy Communion on an average of three times a week. His Holy Cross College number, 17, is retired.

In December 1950, Bob married his college sweetheart, Missie Ritterbusch. Holy Cross Athletic Director Father Tiernan was the celebrant. They had two daughters: Mary Patricia and Marie Colette. They belonged to Blessed Sacrament Parish in Worcester. Bob was a Knight of Columbus. When he was in distress, he appealed to the Blessed Mother. He operated a summer camp for boys, Camp Graylag, outside Pittsfield, Massachusetts.

From 1950 through 1963, Bob played point guard for the Boston Celtics. He was on six championship teams. He was voted to the NBA All-Star Game 13 times. He was the NBA All-Star game Most Valuable Player twice. In 1957, he was the NBA Most Valuable Player. He was the NBA assists leader eight times. From 1954 through 1958, he was the President of the NBA Players Association. He was 6-foot-1; he weighed 175 pounds.

From 1963 through 1969, he coached Boston College. In 1968 and 1969, he was New England Coach of the Year. From 1969 through 1973, he coached the Cincinnati Royals/Kansas City-Omaha Kings.

Bob was a Celtics' broadcaster during the 1980s. He is an NBA Hall of Famer. His Celtics' number, 14, is retired. He was named to the NBA 25th Anniversary Team, the NBA 35thh Anniversary Team, and the NBA 50th Anniversary Team.

Bob's wife, Missie, died in 2013 after 63 years of marriage. He received an honorary doctorate of humane letters from Boston College in 2014. He is a Sports Faith Hall of Famer. On August 22, 2019, he received the Presidential Medal of Freedom.

Terry Brennan

Terence Patrick Brennan was born June 11, 1928 in Milwaukee, Wisconsin. He had three older brothers: Joe, Bill, and Jim. At their home in Whitefish Bay, a suburb of Milwaukee, they practiced the hurdles, the pole vault, and the shot put. Terry was a three-sport athlete (football, hockey, and track) at Marquette University High School.

From 1945 through 1948, Brennan played defensive back and offensive back for the University of Notre Dame. He was president of his sophomore class. In 1947 against the Army Black Knights at Notre Dame, he returned the opening kickoff 97 yards for a touchdown; Notre Dame won 27-7. He started 30 out of 38 games and he played on three undefeated teams. He was 5-foot-11, 160 pounds. He was a philosophy major and he had an 85 average.

From Ed Fitzgerald, we know that, "He went to law school in the mornings; in the afternoons he taught two classes in Accounting at Mt. Carmel High in Chicago and coached the football team. At night, he studied his law books and worked out football plays. In the 4 years he coached at Mt. Carmel, his teams won three successive city championships, something no other school in the city had ever done before."

Brennan went to Mass every day. In June 1953, he earned his law degree from DePaul University. Then he was the University of Notre Dame freshman football coach.

In 1954, after Brennan had been appointed the head football coach at the University of Notre Dame, a reporter pointed out to him that he was only 25 years old. Brennan said, "That's all right. I'll be 26 pretty soon." He was the head coach through the 1958 season.

During spring training in 1959, Brennan was the conditioning coach for the Cincinnati Reds. Then he joined a Chicago investment banking firm. He is in the Chicagoland Sports Hall of Fame, the Wisconsin Athletic Hall of Fame, and the Sports Faith Hall of Fame.

Brennan died on September 7, 2021. He is survived by six children, 27 grandchildren, and 16 great-grandchildren. Brennan's wife, Mary Louise (Kelley) Brennan died in 2001.

Brennan died about the time his new book was published: *Though the Odds Be Great or Small*. The book follows his days as a player at Notre Dame under Frank Leahy and then his coaching career.

Yogi Berra

Lawrence Peter Yogi Berra was born May 12, 1925 in Saint Louis, Missouri. He was Catholic and he attended South Side Catholic. He played American Legion baseball. In 1943, he signed with the New York Yankees. He played for their minor league team in Norfolk, Virginia for one season. During World War II, he served in the Navy. He was awarded a Purple Heart. Then he played for the Newark Bears.

From 1946 through 1963, Yogi played for the Yankees. He was five feet, seven inches tall. He was the

American League Most Valuable Player three times. He was an All-Star 18 times. As a player, he was on 10 championship teams. He is a Hall of Famer. He is on the Major League Baseball All-Century Team. His New York Yankees number, 8, is retired.

In 1964, Yogi was the manager of the Yankees. In 1965, he played for the Mets. From 1965 through 1971, he was a coach for the Mets. From 1972 through 1975, he was the manager of the Mets. From 1976 through 1983, he was a coach of the Yankees. From 1984 through 1985, he was the manager of the Yankees. From 1986 through 1989, he was a coach of the Houston Astros. As a coach, he was on three championship teams.

In January 1949, Yogi met Carmen Short in a Saint Louis restaurant. On January 26, 1949, they got married at Saint Andrew's Church in Saint Louis. They had three sons and they were longtime residents of Montclair, New Jersey. In 1961, Ed Fitzgerald published Yogi's autobiography.

In 1996, Yogi received an honorary doctorate from Montclair State University. In 1998, he opened the Yogi Berra Museum and Learning Center on the campus of Montclair State.

On March 6, 2014, his wife died from a stroke at the age of 88. They were married for 65 years. He died in his sleep of natural causes on September 22, 2015 at the age of 90 in West Caldwell, New Jersey. On November 24, 2015, he was posthumously awarded the Presidential Medal of Freedom.

When Bob Costas spoke at Stan Musial's funeral, he quoted Yogi Berra. "Always go to your friends' funerals, otherwise they won't come to yours."

Stan Musial

Stan Musial was born on November 21, 1920 in Donora, Pennsylvania. He played basketball and baseball for Donora High School. He married his high school sweetheart, Lil Labash, on May 25, 1940 in Daytona Beach, Florida.

Stan was six feet tall and he weighed 175 pounds. He started out as a pitcher, but he finished as an outfielder and a first baseman.

Stan played for the Saint Louis Cardinals baseball team from 1941 through 1944 and from 1946 through 1963. In 1945, he served in the U. S. Navy.

Stan was an All-Star 24 times. He played on three championship teams. He was the National League Most Valuable Player three times. He was the National League batting champion seven times. He was the National League RBI leader twice. His Cardinals' number, 6, is retired. He is in the Saint Louis Cardinals' Hall of Fame, the National Baseball Hall of Fame, and the Sports Faith Hall of Fame.

Stan had 1,815 hits in home games and 1,815 hits in road games. He played in 3,026 games. He was never ejected from a game. Brooklyn Dodgers' fans gave him his nickname, Stan the Man. He was known for his modesty and his sportsmanship.

Here is an excerpt from Ed Fitzgerald's chapter on Stan.

"But the biggest thing about Stan Musial in the minds of the millions of Americans who follow the game closely is that he is a wonderful man. His good nature, his kindness, his clean speech and courteous manner, his amazing modesty in the face of all the adulation that has come his way, are the things one thinks of first in connection with him. Certainly he is a great ballplayer, but a great human being, too."

Stan was named to the Major League Baseball All-Century Team. He received the Presidential Medal of Freedom.

Stan died of natural causes on January 19, 2013, at the age of 92 in Ladue, Missouri. When Bob Costas spoke at Stan's funeral, Bob said that Stan was "thoroughly decent."

Carmen Basilio

Carmen Basilio's father was an immigrant from Italy. Carmen was born April 2, 1927 in Canastota, New York, near Syracuse. He was the seventh of ten children. The Basilio family had an onion farm.

Carmen was on the boxing team at Canastota High School. When he was 17, he enlisted in the Marine Corps. He had overseas duty at Guam and Pearl Harbor. In November 1947, he entered the AAU and Golden Gloves tournaments in Syracuse. Carmen was five feet, six and a half inches tall. On his first date with his wife, he took her to a boxing match.

Ed Fitzgerald wrote this about Carmen. "He rarely argues with anybody and he almost never raises his voice. Despite the fact that he earns his living fighting with his gloved fists in the prize ring, he is a humble man of powerful religious convictions.

"The scrupulously observed ritual of blessing himself before and after each bout is no showoff stunt. Carmen simply wouldn't feel right if he didn't do it, and he doesn't care what anybody thinks about it. 'I know some of them think I'm laying it on,' he says quietly, 'but that doesn't bother me. I'd be bothered only if people thought I was trying to get in good with God just to win the fight. That's not the idea at all. I bless myself before the fight to ask God to keep me from getting badly hurt, and after the fight I do it to thank God for taking care of me. It wouldn't be right to ask Him to help me win; He's got more important things to worry about.'"

On June 10, 1955, Carmen won the world welterweight championship. He won it again on September 12, 1956. On September 23, 1957, he won the world middleweight championship.

After Carmen had retired from boxing, he worked for the Genesee Brewery in Rochester, New York. Then he taught physical education at LeMoyne College in Syracuse. He was also associated with a sausage company.

Carmen is in the International Boxing Hall of Fame. He died on November 7, 2012 in Rochester, New York at the age of 85. He is survived by his wife, four children, and many grandchildren and great grandchildren.

Alex Olmedo

Alex Olmedo was born March 24, 1936, in Arequipa, Peru. He was one of six children. His father, Salvatore, was the caretaker and the pro at the tennis club in Arequipa. He never dreamed that Alex would become the world amateur tennis champion.

When Alex was 14, he was a student at Saint Thomas Aquinas School in Lima. He took a tennis racket out of his father's pro shop. He entered a local men's singles tournament and he won. To pay for the racket, he had jobs around the tennis courts. He took lessons from his father.

Businessmen from Peru raised money to send Alex to the United States. He took a banana boat to Miami. He prayed and asked the blessing of Mamacita, the

Blessed Mother.[42] He helped out as a cabin boy during the three-week journey. He took a bus to Los Angeles.

After Alex had arrived in Los Angeles, he got a job in a tennis club pro shop. He took tennis lessons and he enrolled in night school to learn English. He got a scholarship to Modesto Junior College. He became a member of the Los Angeles Tennis Club.

Alex got a scholarship to the University of Southern California. In the summer of 1956, Alex won the national college championship. In 1958, he won it again; he was also on the winning doubles team.

Alex played on the United States Davis Cup team. He was eligible because he had lived in the U. S. a minimum of 5 years and Peru did not have a Davis Cup team of its own. He won two singles matches and he was on the winning doubles team to help the U. S. obtain victory.

In January of 1959, Alex won the Australian National Championships. When he went back to California, he went back to school. He wrote long letters to his father about how it felt to win the Davis Cup.

From Ed Fitzgerald, we know that, "He was able to thank Mamacita, the Blessed Mother, to whom he had directed all his prayers in those uncertain, homesick, sometimes bitterly discouraging early days in the United States, for all she had done for him. It was quite a lot."

Later in 1959, Alex won the Wimbledon championship. In 1987, he was inducted into the International Tennis Hall of Fame. For over 40 years, he taught tennis at the Beverly Hills Hotel.

He died of brain cancer on December 9, 2020 at the age of 84.

---

[42] Mamacita in English means "little mother" although today is often used to refer to a very attractive woman.

Juan Fangio

Juan Fangio was born June 24, 1911 in Balcarce, Argentina. His father had migrated from Italy to Argentina. He was a potato farmer. Juan was the fourth of six children. When he was in his early teens, he earned money as a mechanic at a local garage.

When Juan was 18, he almost died from pneumonia. Doctors worked urgently to save him. His mother prayed to Our Lady and he recovered.

Juan served in the army at the cadet school, Campo de Mayo, outside of Buenos Aires. He was the chauffeur of the commanding officer.

After the army, Juan wanted to be a racing driver. Balcarce had a plain dirt track that had automobile races. He started out as an assistant driver because he could be a mechanic if there was trouble.

When he was 23, he got to drive his first race. He did not finish because his car was a rebuilt taxicab that fell apart at the halfway point.

Juan built a car of his own with parts from three different cars. The rear axle was from a Buick. The transmission was from a Chevrolet. The engine block was from a Ford. He always did his best even though he didn't win a race for a long time.

He said, "You must always do your best, but you must never believe that you are."

When he was 29, he had his first victory. It was the 1940 Gran Premio Internacional del Norte. He drove 5,932 miles from Buenos Aires to Lima and back. After the race, he went back to Balcarce and set up a car dealership. He was successful as a race driver and as a businessman. During World War II, there weren't car races, but he kept the town's cars running. When money was scarce, he was a taxicab driver.

Juan won the Formula One World Championships in 1951, 1954, 1955, 1956, and 1957.

After he had been kidnapped before a race in Cuba, he became a friend to the men who had captured him.

After he had retired from racing, Juan sold Mercedes-Benz cars. In 1990, he was inducted into the International Motorsports Hall of Fame. On July 17, 1995, he died in Buenos Aires at the age of 84 from kidney failure and pneumonia.

Ron Delany

Ronald Michael Delany was born on March 6, 1935 in Arklow, Ireland. When he was five, he moved with his family to Dublin. He went to the O'Connell School and then to Catholic University School.

In high school, Ron played tennis, rugby, field hockey, and cricket. He also ran track.

In September 1954, he went to Villanova University, near Philadelphia, on a track scholarship. He earned five dollars a week by directing traffic at the Saint Thomas Church Sunday Masses.

From Ed Fitzgerald, we know that Ron preferred track to any other sport. Ron said, "Track, and track alone provides the opportunity to compete on an equal basis, man against man. In tennis, for example, there is a margin for error in a bad racket that gives one man an unfair advantage over another. There is an acquired technical skill essential in handling a weapon in many sports. If your grip is not proper, you're at a disadvantage. In Rugby, you depend upon the other fourteen men for success. In track, however, it is you, stripped down, all by yourself, against your opponents. Nobody brings any help or any weapons into the contest. You're on your own, against the field."

Ron was 5-foot-11. He weighed 150 pounds. In the 1956 Summer Olympics in Melbourne, Australia, he won the gold medal in the 1500 meters run.

Ron studied commerce and finance at Villanova. He wore a miraculous medal and a scapular. He also went to graduate school there. When he was in Ireland, he visited crippled children at Saint Mary's Hospital in Cappagh. When it was raining, he quoted Dubliners. "It's a fine, soft night, thanks be to God. Truthfully, there are no bad days in Dublin."

Ron had four AAU titles, four Irish national titles, and three NCAA titles. In indoor track, he had a 40-race winning streak. He broke the world indoor mile record three times.

After he had retired from competition, he worked for the Irish airline Aer Lingus and the Irish Ferry Company in Dublin. In 2006, he received an honorary Doctor of Laws Degree from University College Dublin.

Eddie Arcaro

George Edward Arcaro was born on February 19, 1916 in Cincinnati. He grew up in Newport, Kentucky. He insisted that he wanted to be a jockey. He started out by sweeping the stables, cleaning the equipment, and walking the horses to cool them off after their workouts.

When Eddie was 15, he went to Agua Caliente, Mexico. He rode in almost a hundred races before he got his first victory. It was on January 14, 1932.

Then Eddie went to Sportsman's Park in Chicago. In one week he rode fourteen winners. In New Orleans, he rode 43 winners.

From Ed Fitzgerald, we know that "A good jockey is much more than a rider; he is an athlete. He has to have perfect balance, strong legs to sit properly on the horse and grip him tightly with knees and shins, and powerful wrists to control the reins and the horse's head.

"By any standard, Eddie Arcaro is a thumping success, and he has made it because he has the three things a man in his occupation must have—skill, courage, and the will to win. In any occupation, that combination is unbeatable."

Eddie won the Kentucky Derby five times. He won the Preakness Stakes six times. He won the Belmont Stakes six times. He was the Triple Crown winner twice. He had 4,779 career wins. His autobiography is entitled, *I Ride to Win*. He was 5-foot-3. He weighed 108 pounds.

In 1958, Eddie was inducted into the United States Racing Hall of Fame in Saratoga Springs, New York. In 1962, he retired from racing. He was a racing television commentator, a public relations officer for a casino, a car spokesman, and a restaurant proprietor. Then he and his first wife, Ruth, settled in South Florida. He played golf daily and he analyzed races for television. They were married for 50 years until she died in 1988. They had two children, Carolyn and Bobby. In 1996, he married a long-time friend, Vera.

On November 14, 1997, he died in Miami at the age of 81 of liver cancer. He was interred in Our Lady of Mercy Catholic Cemetery in Miami.

Jean Beliveau

Jean Beliveau was born August 31, 1931 in Trois-Rivieres, Quebec, Canada. He was the oldest of eight children. When Jean was six, he moved with his family to Victoriaville. He went to L'Ecole Saint-David, L'Academie Saint-Louis, and College deVictoriaville.

From Ed Fitzgerald, we know that "In Three Rivers, the French-Canadian town in the province of Quebec where Jean Beliveau was born, the kids play hockey on the frozen ponds and lakes until their ears and noses and cheeks are bright red with the cold. Even when the drifting snow piles deep on the ice, they borrow shovels from their fathers and brooms from their mothers and clear enough space for at least a compressed version of the game. They play from eight in the morning until six in the evening, taking only the briefest of rest periods for a lunch that usually consists only of a half-frozen sandwich brought to the lake in a paper bag and always eaten with the skates still on. By the time these boys grow to be sturdy teen-agers, they are experienced hockey players."

Jean played amateur hockey in the Quebec Senior Hockey League. In the summers, he played baseball. He was a pitcher and an infielder. When he was 15, he turned down a minor league baseball contract.

In 1950, he met Elise Couture in Quebec City. On June 27, 1953, they got married at Saint Patrick's Church there. They had one daughter, Helene, and two granddaughters, Mylene and Magalie.

From 1953 through 1971, Jean played for the Montreal Canadiens. He was 6-foot-3, 205 pounds. He played center. On October 9, 1971, his jersey number, 4, was retired. In 1972, he was inducted into the Hockey Hall of Fame. He was on 10 Canadiens championship teams as a player and seven as an executive. He was a vice president and director of public relations.

Jean started a foundation that later was transferred to the Society for Disabled Children. Among many honors, he was knighted in the National Order of Quebec. His name was added to Canada's Walk of Fame. His portrait was on a Canadian postage stamp. On December 2, 2014, he died in Longueuil, a suburb of

Montreal, at the age of 83. His funeral was at Mary Queen of the World Cathedral in Montreal.

Herb Score

Herbert Jude Score was born on June 7, 1933 in Rosedale, New York. When he was three, a truck ran over his legs. A few months later, he was in bed with rheumatic fever. Jude was his Confirmation name. He wore a Saint Jude medal around his neck.

When Herb was a high school freshman, he had a fractured ankle. While he was in a cast, he had surgery for appendicitis. He had pneumonia twice, a colon condition, high blood pressure, and a separated left shoulder.

From Ed Fitzgerald, we know that "Herb played the outfield and first base for Holy Name of Mary School until the coach, Father Thomas Kelly, notified him that he would be better off pitching. Father Kelly, an old Fordham shortstop, sensed that he could always get hold of an adequate outfielder or first baseman, but he would wait a long time for another pitcher like Herb Score." He also played basketball there.

Then Herb moved with his family to Lake Worth, Florida. In 1952, Lake Worth High School won the Florida state championship. Herb threw six no-hitters.

On June 7, 1952, his 19th birthday, he signed with the Cleveland Indians. He pitched for Indianapolis of the American Association. In 1953, he pitched for Reading, Pennsylvania of the Eastern League. In 1954, he pitched for Triple-A Indianapolis. He was the Minor League Player of the Year.

In 1955, he pitched for the Cleveland Indians. He was the American League Rookie of the Year and an All-Star. In 1956, he was an All-Star again.

TUITION REBATE

On May 7, 1957, Herb was hit in the face with a batted ball. In July he married his long-time sweetheart, Nancy McNamara. Then he returned to Cleveland for workouts. He pitched for the Indians in 1958 and 1959. From 1960 through 1962, he pitched for the Chicago White Sox.

Herb was a broadcaster for the Indians from 1964 through 1997. He is in the Broadcasters Hall of Fame. On November 11, 2008, he died at his home in Rocky River, Ohio at the age of 75. He is interred at Lakewood Park Cemetery in Rocky River.

PHOTOS AND ILLUSTRATIONS

All photographs are reproduced with permission (unless public domain).

Page	Description	Source
Front Cover	Michael McCaskey and Fiche Ethiopia Students, Peace Corps	Chicago Bears Football Club
Page vi	Patrick McCaskey	Chicago Bears Football Club
Page 2	Michael McCaskey and Fiche Ethiopia Students, Peace Corps	Chicago Bears Football Club
Page 10	Molly Seidel	University of Notre Dame Athletic Department
Page 19	Monument to Henry Wadsworth Longfellow in Portland, Maine's, Longfellow Square	Carol Highsmith, Library of Congress
Page 32	Biese Family	Nikki Biese
Page 65	Bill Potter illustration.	From *Baseball's Winning Ways* published by Sporting Chance Press
Page 66	Gale Sayers speaks to the troops at an USO show on Bagram Air Field, Afghanistan	U. S. Army photo taken by Spc. Joshua Balog, accessed from Wikimedia Commons.

Page	Description	Source
Page 70	Dick Hoyt, John Kerry, Bryan Lyons, and Rick Hoyt	U. S. State Department Photo, accessed from Wikimedia Commons.
Page 74	Tommie Harris on USO tour at Manas Air Base in Kyrgyzstan signs an autograph for Senior Master Sgt. Marc Pumala, 376th Expeditionary Security Forces Squadron.	U. S. Air Force, photo by U.S. Air Force, Senior Airman Tabitha Kuykendall accessed from Wikimedia Commons
Page 79	Patrick McCaskey at WSFI radio studio.	WSFI Catholic Radio
Page 104	Principal Dan Tully	Notre Dame College Prep
Page 132	WPA Poster, Back to Books	Library of Congress
Page 154	Bill Potter illustration.	From *Pillars of the NFL* published by Sporting Chance Press
Page 164	Photo by Carol Highsmith, Library of Congress Reading Room	Library of Congress
Back Cover	Patrick McCaskey in studio and graduation scene.	WSFI Catholic Radio and Notre Dame College Prep

INDEX

TUITION REBATE

Patrick McCaskey

TUITION REBATE

Patrick McCaskey

Patrick McCaskey was born at Saint Francis Hospital in Evanston. He played basketball and baseball for Saint Mary's School in Des Plaines; he played football and ran track for Notre Dame High School in Niles; and he ran cross-country and track for Cheshire Academy in Connecticut.

A contributing editor to the literary magazines at Loyola University in Chicago and Indiana University, Pat started working for the Chicago Bears in 1974. Encouraged by his grandfather, George Halas, he attended DePaul University at night during the off-seasons and earned a master's degree in the interdisciplinary studies of business, writing, and performing.

Pat is a Chicago Bears' Board Member and a Bears' Vice President. He is the Chairman of Sports Faith International which recognizes people who are successful in sports while leading exemplary lives. Sports Faith has a radio station, WSFI, 88.5 FM, which broadcasts in northern Illinois and southern Wisconsin. Pat and his wife, Gretchen, have three sons: Ed, Tom, and Jim; two daughters-in-law: Elizabeth and Emily; four granddaughters: Grace, Charlotte, Violet Min, and Madeline; and one grandson, Pat.